MW00697246

Vocabulary Building Practice and Apply: Grade 7

BY
MARILYN K. SMITH AND VICTORIA QUIGLEY FORBES

COPYRIGHT © 2001 Mark Twain Media, Inc.

ISBN 1-58037-158-2

Printing No. CD-1379

Mark Twain Media, Inc., Publishers
Distributed by Carson-Dellosa Publishing Company, Inc.

Table of Contents

Letter to the Teacher

Vocabulary words are an important part of our language; they are a part of our everyday listening, reading, and writing. Vocabulary words are often categorized to help with student learning. Student comprehension of vocabulary meaning is heightened when the words are related to a certain topic or theme. Each unit in this book includes a list of vocabulary words based on one letter of the alphabet.

Each unit incorporates an *Introductory* page, a *Get the Facts* page, a *Skills and Practice* page, and a *Vocabulary Quiz*.

Introduction - This page includes a list of vocabulary words and pronunciations for the unit. There is also an exercise for the student to alphabetize the words for that unit. This page will help the teacher introduce the words and further develop the students' skills in alphabetizing.

Get the Facts - This page is intended for each student's use in learning the meaning of each word and as a resource for the *Skills and Practice* page that follows.

Skills and Practice - All units include synonym, antonym, and/or categorizing activities. These allow the student to show mastery of the meaning of the words as well as to generate new related words. There are also activities to help take the student beyond the meaning of the words in the "Extend Your Vocabulary" section.

Vocabulary Quiz - This page may be used to test the students' knowledge of the words.

All units can be used either together or separately. The back of the book includes a list of additional vocabulary words. There are also forms that can be used with any unit and any vocabulary word. A list page, Venn diagram, and T-chart are also included for use along with the various "Extend Your Vocabulary" activities.

Criteria for the vocabulary words selected for this book included *The Basic Skills Word List, The New Reading Teachers Book of Lists, Words to Use for Sentence Building*, and numerous thesauruses. Words were most importantly chosen based on the word's appropriateness to grade level and lesson. A combination of 40 years of teaching at this grade level by the authors of this book contributed to the selection of the words as well.

Pronunciation Key

a	hat	îr	here	o͝o	look, put	ch	child
ā	age	ī	ice	o͞o	tool	ng	long
ä	far	i	it	ou	out	sh	she
e	let	o	hot	oi	oil	th	thin
ē	equal	ō	open	u	cup	*th*	those
ėr	term	ô	law, order	ū, yo͞o	use	zh	measure
âr	care			ü	rule		

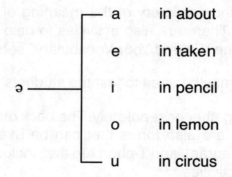

ə   a   in about
     e   in taken
     i   in pencil
     o   in lemon
     u   in circus

Name: _____   Date: _____

Unit 6: "F" Words: *Vocabulary List and Alphabetizing*

filament   folly   fallacy

fascinate (fas´ ə nāt´)	feeble (fē´ bəl)
filth (filth)	furthermore (fûr´ *th*ər môr´)
falsehood (fôls´ hŏod)	falter (fôl´ tər)
fiancée (fē´ än sā´)	fiend (fēnd)
folly (fol´ ē)	forlorn (fôr lôrn´)
filament (fil´ ə mənt)	fumigate (fyōō´ mə gāt´)
fictitious (fik tish´ əs)	forum (fôr´ əm)
froth (frôth)	fallacy (fal´ ə sē)
fervent (fer´ vənt)	fraudulent (frô´ jə lənt)
frivolous (friv´ ə ləs)	futile (fyōō´ tl)

Directions: Write the above vocabulary words in alphabetical order below.

1. _____   11. _____
2. _____   12. _____
3. _____   13. _____
4. _____   14. _____
5. _____   15. _____
6. _____   16. _____
7. _____   17. _____
8. _____   18. _____
9. _____   19. _____
10. _____   20. _____

Unit 6: "F" Words: *Get the Facts!*

fascinate (fas´ ə nāt´) attract very strongly; enchant by charming qualities; charm. *The preschoolers were fascinated with the dinosaur exhibit.*

feeble (fē´ bəl) lacking strength; weak. *The feeble child was resting after surgery.*

filth (filth) foul dirt; refuse. *The filth in the park was cleaned up by the school group as a service project.*

furthermore (fûr´ *th*ər môr´) in addition; moreover; also. *Furthermore, the report will be due on Tuesday.*

falsehood (fôls´ hŏod) false statement; lie. *The falsehood was the reason for her punishment.*

falter (fôl´ tər) not go straight on; draw back or hesitate. *I faltered on my decision to skydive.*

fiancée (fē´ än sā´) woman engaged to be married. *My fiancée was to meet me at the restaurant at 6:00 P.M.*

fiend (fēnd) evil spirit; very wicked or cruel person. *She was a fiend toward the rest of her family.*

folly (fol´ ē) being foolish; lack of sense; unwise conduct. *It was folly to try to cross the high waters.*

forlorn (fôr lôrn´) miserable and hopeless from being left alone and neglected. *The forlorn puppy needed a good home.*

filament (fil´ ə mənt) very fine thread; very slender, threadlike part. *The filament in the light bulb was damaged.*

fumigate (fyoo´ mə gāt´) disinfect with fumes. *We will need to fumigate the building to destroy the roaches.*

fictitious (fik tish´ əs) not real; imaginary. *She used a fictitious name for the newspaper article.*

forum (fôr´ əm) assembly for the discussion of questions of public interest. *A public forum for the candidates will be held in the auditorium.*

froth (frôth) mass of very small bubbles formed in liquid. *The froth on the edge of the wave could be seen from the shore.*

fallacy (fal´ ə sē) false idea; mistaken belief; error. *Some home remedies are a fallacy and do not work.*

fervent (fer´ vənt) showing great warmth of feeling; very earnest. *He made a fervent request for money for the orphanage.*

fraudulent (frô´ jə lənt) cheating; dishonest. *He was a fraudulent player and did not win honestly.*

frivolous (friv´ ə ləs) lacking in seriousness or sense; silly. *Her frivolous behavior in school got her into trouble.*

futile (fyoo´ tl) not successful; useless. *His efforts to win the race were futile.*

Name: _____   Date: _____

Unit 6: "F" Words: *Skills and Practice*

Directions: Write a **synonym** from the list of vocabulary words below on the line. A **synonym** is a word that means the same or nearly the same.

fascinate	**falter**	**fervent**	**frivolous**	**furthermore**
fumigate	**froth**	**futile**		

1. waver _____
2. charm _____
3. foam _____
4. also _____
5. useless _____
6. disinfect _____
7. silly _____
8. passionate _____

> **Did You Know?** A fiancée is a woman engaged to be married, and a fiancé is a man engaged to be married.

Directions: Write an **antonym** from the list of vocabulary words below on the line. An **antonym** is a word that means the opposite or nearly opposite.

filth	**feeble**	**fictitious**	**falsehood**	**fraudulent**
folly	**forlorn**			

1. strong _____
2. truth _____
3. clean _____
4. real _____
5. honest _____
6. hopeful _____
7. wise _____

Directions: Write a sentence for each of the vocabulary words below on your own paper. Remember to check your spelling and punctuation.

fiancée	**fiend**	**forum**	**fallacy**

Extend Your Vocabulary

1. Make a Venn diagram comparing the use of a forum in the Greek and Roman civilizations.
2. Write a narrative piece about a time when you were fascinated.
3. Make a list of things you would consider to be frivolous. Compare with a partner.
4. Write a descriptive paragraph about a fictitious character you have read about. Include many vivid adjectives.

Name: _____ Date: _____

Unit 6: "F" Words: *Vocabulary Quiz*

Directions: Match each vocabulary word with the correct meaning. Write the word on the line next to the meaning.

fascinate	feeble	filth	furthermore	falsehood
falter	fiancée	fiend	fumigate	forlorn
frivolous	filament	folly	fictitious	forum
froth	fallacy	fervent	fraudulent	futile

1. _____ disinfect with fumes

2. _____ foul dirt; refuse

3. _____ mass of very small bubbles formed in liquid

4. _____ evil spirit; very wicked or cruel person

5. _____ cheating; dishonest

6. _____ miserable and hopeless from being left alone and neglected

7. _____ very fine thread; very slender; threadlike part

8. _____ attract very strongly; enchant by charming qualities; charm

9. _____ not real; imaginary

10. _____ in addition; moreover; also

11. _____ false idea; mistaken belief; error

12. _____ not go straight on; draw back or hesitate

13. _____ not successful; useless

14. _____ being foolish; lack of sense; unwise conduct

15. _____ assembly for the discussion of questions of public interest

16. _____ lacking strength; weak

17. _____ showing great warmth of feeling; very earnest

18. _____ false statement; lie

19. _____ lacking in seriousness or sense; silly

20. _____ woman engaged to be married

Name: _____ Date: _____

Unit 7: "G" Words: *Vocabulary List and Alphabetizing*

gamut

garish

gusto

gaiety

genuine (jen´ yo͞o ən)

gale (gāl)

gaiety (gā´ ə tē)

gallows (gal´ ōz)

genial (jē´ nyəl)

gaunt (gônt)

grimace (grim´ is)

gusto (gus´ tō)

gamut (gam´ ət)

genuflect (jen´ yə flekt´)

guarantee (gar´ ən tē´)

gruff (gruf)

gruesome (gro͞o´ səm)

galvanize (gal´ və nīz)

glutton (glut´ ən)

genteel (jen tēl´)

grotesque (grō tesk´)

gainsay (gān´ sā´)

garish (gār´ ish)

gibberish (jib´ ər ish)

Directions: Write the above vocabulary words in alphabetical order below.

1. _____   11. _____

2. _____   12. _____

3. _____   13. _____

4. _____   14. _____

5. _____   15. _____

6. _____   16. _____

7. _____   17. _____

8. _____   18. _____

9. _____   19. _____

10. _____   20. _____

Unit 7: "G" Words: *Get the Facts!*

genuine (jen´ yoo ən) actually being what it seems or is claimed to be; real; sincere. *The girl was genuine in wishing luck to her competitors.*

guarantee (gar´ ən tē´) promise or pledge to replace or repair a purchased product or to return the money paid, if unsatisfactory. *A product guarantee came with our new washing machine.*

gale (gāl) very strong wind. *A gale can blow up to 63 miles an hour.*

gruff (gruf) deep and harsh; hoarse. *As a result of the man's cold, his voice sounded gruff.*

gaiety (gā´ ə tē) cheerful liveliness; joyousness. *She could not hide her gaiety after winning the competition.*

gruesome (groo´ səm) causing fear or horror; horrible; revolting. *The gruesome Halloween mask scared the children.*

gallows (gal´ ōz) wooden frame constructed of a crossbar on two upright posts, used for hanging criminals. *A gallows was used in the Old West to punish cattle rustlers.*

galvanize (gal´ və nīz) to stimulate as if by electric shock; startle; to plate metal with zinc. *The man was galvanized by the ringing alarm.*

genial (jē´ nyəl) smiling and pleasant; cheerful and friendly. *They gave us a genial welcome as we entered the door.*

glutton (glut´ ən) person who never seems to have enough of something. *He was a glutton when it came to eating sweets.*

gaunt (gônt) pinched and lean; harsh or forlorn in appearance. *Her illness left the woman looking gaunt.*

genteel (jen tēl´) polite; well-bred; fashionable; elegant. *Her genteel appearance seemed out of place at the noisy ballpark.*

grimace (grim´ is) twisting or distortion of the face; ugly or funny smile. *A grimace crossed her face because of the pain.*

grotesque (grō tesk´) odd or unnatural in shape, appearance, or manner; odd. *The grotesque costume won the contest at the Halloween party.*

gusto (gus´ tō) hearty enjoyment. *The family ate the special dinner with gusto.*

gainsay (gān´ sā´) deny; contradict; dispute. *She tried to gainsay his opinion with her own.*

gamut (gam´ ət) the whole range of anything. *The actress's audition included a gamut of emotions and facial expressions.*

garish (gār´ ish) unpleasantly bright; glaring; gaudy. *The garish outfit she wore to the formal dinner brought many stares.*

genuflect (jen´ yə flekt´) bend the knee as an act of reverence or worship. *She was taught to genuflect as she entered the church.*

gibberish (jib´ ər ish) senseless chatter; confused, meaningless talk or writing. *The baby's gibberish could be heard from the other room.*

Unit 7: "G" Words: *Skills and Practice*

Directions: Write a **synonym** from the list of vocabulary words below on the line. A **synonym** is a word that means the same or nearly the same.

grotesque	gibberish	grimace	gruesome	gruff
galvanize	genuine	genial	guarantee	gaunt

1. jabber _____
2. revolting _____
3. friendly _____
4. hoarse _____
5. startle _____
6. authentic _____
7. desolate _____
8. warranty _____
9. distorted _____
10. odd _____

> **Did You Know?** The Greek root *gen* means "birth" or "race," as in *generation, genocide,* and *genealogy.*

Directions: Write an **antonym** from the list of vocabulary words below on the line. An **antonym** is a word that means the opposite or nearly opposite.

gaiety	garish	gainsay	genteel	gusto

1. impolite _____
2. seriousness _____
3. dissatisfaction _____
4. plain _____
5. affirm _____

Directions: Write a sentence for each of the vocabulary words below on your own paper. Remember to check your spelling and punctuation.

genuflect	gamut	glutton	gale	gallows

Extend Your Vocabulary

1. Make a list of garish things.
2. Write a persuasive piece about why companies should or should not guarantee things.
3. Compare a tornado to a gale. Include size, speed, and destruction.
4. Write an expository piece about how you can tell if someone is being genuine.

Name: _____ Date: _____

Unit 7: "G" Words: *Vocabulary Quiz*

Directions: Match each vocabulary word with the correct meaning. Write the word on the line next to the meaning.

genuine	**guarantee**	**grotesque**	**gruff**	**gaiety**
gruesome	**gallows**	**galvanize**	**genial**	**glutton**
gibberish	**genteel**	**grimace**	**gale**	**gusto**
gainsay	**genuflect**	**garish**	**gamut**	**gaunt**

1. _____ actually being what it seems or is claimed to be; real; sincere

2. _____ deny; contradict; dispute

3. _____ wooden frame constructed of a crossbar on two upright posts, used for hanging

4. _____ senseless chatter; confused, meaningless talk or writing

5. _____ cheerful liveliness; joyousness

6. _____ twisting or distortion of the face; ugly or funny smile

7. _____ polite; well-bred; fashionable; elegant

8. _____ hearty enjoyment

9. _____ very strong wind

10. _____ odd or unnatural in shape, appearance, or manner; odd

11. _____ causing fear or horror; horrible; revolting

12. _____ bend the knee as an act of reverence or worship

13. _____ person who never seems to have enough of something

14. _____ whole range of anything

15. _____ promise or pledge to replace or repair a purchased product or to return the money paid, if unsatisfactory

16. _____ unpleasantly bright; glaring; gaudy

17. _____ deep and harsh; hoarse

18. _____ pinched and lean; harsh or forlorn in appearance

19. _____ smiling and pleasant; cheerful and friendly

20. _____ to stimulate as if by electric shock; startle; to plate with zinc

Name: _____   Date: _____

Unit 8: "H" Words: *Vocabulary List and Alphabetizing*

horticulture (hôr´ tə kul´ chər)   humane (hyōo mān´)

haughty (hôt´ ē)   hoard (hôrd)

heirloom (er´ lōom)   hideous (hid´ ē əs)

homage (hom´ ij)   hypocrite (hip´ ə krit)

hysteria (hi ster´ ē ə)   hallucination (hə lōo´ si nā´ shən)

haphazard (hap´ haz´ ərd)   herbivorous (hər biv´ ər əs)

hindrance (hin´ drəns)   hypertension (hī´ pər ten´ shən)

hypertrophy (hī pûr´ trə fē)   hypochondria (hī´ pə kon´ drē ə)

hypotenuse (hī pot´ 'n ōos´)   hypodermic (hī´ pə dûr´ mik)

hypothesis (hī poth´ ə sis)   hypoglycemia (hī´ pō glī sē´ mē ə)

Directions: Write the above vocabulary words in alphabetical order below.

1. _____   11. _____

2. _____   12. _____

3. _____   13. _____

4. _____   14. _____

5. _____   15. _____

6. _____   16. _____

7. _____   17. _____

8. _____   18. _____

9. _____   19. _____

10. _____   20. _____

Unit 8: "H" Words: *Get the Facts!*

horticulture (hôr´ tə kul´ chər) art or science of growing flowers, fruits, vegetables, and shrubs, especially in a garden or orchard. *The beauty of his extensive gardens showcased his interest in horticulture.*

humane (hyoō mān´) not cruel or brutal; kind; merciful. *The humane society was hoping to raise money for the shelter.*

haughty (hôt´ ē) too proud of oneself and too scornful of others. *The haughty child was not well-liked.*

hoard (hôrd) save and store away. *The squirrel hoarded the nuts for winter.*

heirloom (er´ loōm) possession handed down from generation to generation. *The quilt is a family heirloom.*

hideous (hid´ ē əs) very ugly; frightful; horrible. *The boy's frightening Halloween mask looked hideous to the children.*

homage (hom´ ij) dutiful respect; reverence; honor. *The people paid homage to their leader.*

hypocrite (hip´ ə krit) person who is not sincere; pretender. *The hypocrite pretended to be concerned about the tragic accident.*

hysteria (hi ster´ ē ə) a mental illness caused by anxiety or worry. *A person suffering from hysteria may cry uncontrollably.*

hallucination (hə loō´ si nā´ shən) seeing or hearing things that exist only in a person's imagination. *In spite of her parents' reassurances that her hallucinations weren't real, the little girl was still afraid to go back to sleep.*

haphazard (hap´ haz´ ərd) not planned; random. *The celebration party was thrown together in a haphazard way.*

herbivorous (hər biv´ ər əs) feeding on grass or other plants. *A horse is a herbivorous animal.*

hindrance (hin´ drəns) person or thing that hinders; obstacle. *The noisy party was a hindrance when trying to quiet the child.*

hypertension (hī´ pər ten´ shən) abnormally high blood pressure. *His hypertension was a concern for everyone.*

hypertrophy (hī pûr´ trə fē) enlargement of a body part or organ. *The hypertrophy of the liver was causing the problem.*

hypochondria (hī´ pə kon´ drē ə) abnormal anxiety over one's health; imaginary illness. *The woman suffered from hypochondria and missed work often.*

hypotenuse (hī pot´ 'n oōs´) the side of a right triangle opposite the right angle. *We used a protractor to find the hypotenuse of the triangle.*

hypodermic (hī´ pə dûr´ mik) under the skin. *The hypodermic needle was used by the doctor to give his patient a flu shot.*

hypothesis (hī poth´ ə sis) something assumed because it seems likely to be a true explanation; theory. *We will test our hypothesis by conducting an experiment.*

hypoglycemia (hī´ pō glī sē´ mē ə) condition caused by a lowered level of sugar in the blood, usually because of the presence of too much insulin. *He has known about his hypoglycemia for only a year and is careful about his diet.*

Name: _____   Date: _____

Unit 8: "H" Words: *Skills and Practice*

Directions: Write a **synonym** from the list of vocabulary words below on the line. A **synonym** is a word that means the same or nearly the same.

haughty	**hypocrite**	**hideous**	**heirloom**	**hypothesis**
hindrance	**hallucination**	**hoard**	**homage**	

1. horrible _____
2. arrogant _____
3. obstacle _____
4. pretender _____
5. save _____
6. inheritance _____
7. delusion _____
8. reverence _____
9. supposition _____

> **Did You Know?** The prefix *hypo-* means "too little" or "under." The prefix *hyper-* means "excessive."

Directions: Write an **antonym** from the list of vocabulary words below on the line. An **antonym** is a word that means the opposite or nearly opposite.

herbivorous	**haphazard**	**hysteria**	**humane**

1. planned _____
2. cruel _____
3. carnivorous _____
4. sanity _____

Directions: Write a sentence for each of the vocabulary words below on your own paper. Remember to check your spelling and punctuation.

hypertension	**hypertrophy**	**hypochondria**	**hypotenuse**
hypodermic	**hypoglycemia**	**horticulture**	

Extend Your Vocabulary

1. Make a list of animals that are herbivorous.
2. Contact or visit the humane society in your town. Ask them about volunteering and tell your class about it.
3. Research hypochondria. Describe the characteristics of a hypochondriac.
4. Write a mini-report on hypertension.

31

Name: _____ Date: _____

Unit 8: "H" Words: *Vocabulary Quiz*

Directions: Match each vocabulary word with the correct meaning. Write the word on the line next to the meaning.

horticulture	humane	haughty	herbivorous	heirloom
hypodermic	homage	hypocrite	hypotenuse	hallucination
haphazard	hoard	hindrance	hypertension	hypertrophy
hypochondria	hysteria	hideous	hypothesis	hypoglycemia

1. _____ person or thing that hinders; obstacle

2. _____ not cruel or brutal; kind; merciful

3. _____ something assumed because it seems likely to be a true explanation; theory

4. _____ seeing or hearing things that exist only in a person's imagination

5. _____ feeding on grass or other plants

6. _____ art or science of growing flowers, fruits, vegetables, or shrubs, especially in a garden or orchard

7. _____ an abnormally high blood pressure

8. _____ very ugly; frightful; horrible

9. _____ abnormal anxiety over one's health; imaginary illness

10. _____ person who is not sincere; pretender

11. _____ under the skin

12. _____ not planned; random

13. _____ enlargement of a body part or organ

14. _____ save and store away

15. _____ condition caused by a lowered level of sugar in the blood, usually because of the presence of too much insulin

16. _____ possession handed down from generation to generation

17. _____ the side of a right triangle opposite the right angle

18. _____ mental illness caused by anxiety or worry

19. _____ too proud of oneself and too scornful of others

20. _____ dutiful respect; reverence; honor

Name: _____ Date: _____

Unit 9: "I" Words: *Vocabulary List and Alphabetizing*

immense (i mens´)

inflammable (in flam´ ə bəl)

intrigue (in trēg´)

infantry (in´ fən trē)

illustrious (i lus´ trē əs)

innumerable (in nōō´ mer ə bəl)

instigate (in´ stə gāt´)

illiterate (i lit´ ər it)

imperil (im per´ əl)

insinuate (in sin´ yōō āt´)

impose (im pōz´)

infuriate (in fyŏŏr´ ē āt)

indelible (in del´ ə bəl)

instantaneous (in´ stən tā´ nē əs)

impertinent (im pûrt´ 'n ənt)

inclination (in´ klə nā´ shən)

inevitable (in ev´ i tə bəl)

immaterial (im´ ə tir´ ē əl)

impudent (im´ pyōō dənt)

indispensable (in´ di spen´ sə bəl)

Directions: Write the above vocabulary words in alphabetical order below.

1. _____   11. _____

2. _____   12. _____

3. _____   13. _____

4. _____   14. _____

5. _____   15. _____

6. _____   16. _____

7. _____   17. _____

8. _____   18. _____

9. _____   19. _____

10. _____   20. _____

Unit 9: "I" Words: *Get the Facts!*

immense (i mens´) very large; huge; vast. *The immense body of water could be seen from the plane.*

impose (im pōz´) force or thrust one's authority or influence on another. *The ruler tried to impose new laws on his country.*

inflammable (in flam´ ə bəl) easily excited or aroused; excitable. *He was known for his inflammable temper.*

infuriate (in fyŏŏr´ ē āt) fill with wild, fierce anger; make furious. *The injustice of the verdict infuriated the crowd.*

intrigue (in trēg´) excite the curiosity and interest of. *We were intrigued by the magician's tricks.*

indelible (in del´ ə bəl) not able to be erased or removed. *The indelible ink ruined the lacy tablecloth when it spilled.*

infantry (in´ fən trē) soldiers trained, equipped, and organized to fight on foot. *The infantry was prepared to leave at a moment's notice.*

instantaneous (in´ stən tā´ nē əs) coming or done in an instant. *The response of the community to aid the victims of the flood was instantaneous.*

illustrious (i lus´ trē əs) very famous; great; outstanding. *The illustrious leader led them to victory.*

impertinent (im pûrt´ 'n ənt) not pertinent; not to the point; out of place. *The impertinent information was of no use to the investigation.*

innumerable (in nōō´ mer ə bəl) cannot be counted; very numerous. *There are innumerable ways in which people can help their communities.*

inclination (in´ klə nā´ shən) natural bent; tendency. *The mother's inclination was to be overly concerned regarding her children.*

instigate (in´ stə gāt´) urge on; stir up. *The older of the two brothers instigated the argument.*

inevitable (in ev´ i tə bəl) not to be avoided; sure to happen. *The rain was inevitable, so the picnic was changed to indoors.*

illiterate (i lit´ ər it) not knowing how to read and write. *She was not able to fill out the job application because she was illiterate.*

immaterial (im´ ə tir´ ē əl) not important; insignificant. *The judge ruled that the evidence was immaterial to the crime.*

imperil (im per´ əl) put in danger. *Playing with matches imperils a child's life.*

impudent (im´ pyōō dənt) shamelessly bold; very rude. *The impudent boy earned a detention from his teacher.*

insinuate (in sin´ yōō āt´) suggest in an indirect way. *She insinuated I had the wrong answer on my paper.*

indispensable (in´ di spen´ sə bəl) absolutely necessary. *The firefighters' efforts were indispensable in saving the people from the burning building.*

Name: _____ Date: _____

Unit 9: "I" Words: *Skills and Practice*

Directions: Write a **synonym** from the list of vocabulary words below on the line. A **synonym** is a word that means the same or nearly the same.

insinuate	**inflammable**	**immense**	**indelible**	**innumerable**
illustrious	**inevitable**	**infuriate**	**inclination**	

1. vast _____   2. enrage _____

3. outstanding _____   4. tendency _____

5. excitable _____   6. certain _____

7. permanent _____   8. hint _____

9. countless _____

> **Did You Know?** The prefixes *im-, in-,* and *il-* mean "not," as in *imbalance, inaccurate,* and *illegal.*

Directions: Write an **antonym** from the list of vocabulary words below on the line. An **antonym** is a word that means the opposite or nearly opposite.

indispensable	**intrigue**	**instantaneous**	**immaterial**	**impudent**

1. prolonged _____   2. unnecessary _____

3. polite _____   4. bore _____

5. important _____

Directions: Write a sentence for each of the vocabulary words below on your own paper. Remember to check your spelling and punctuation.

impertinent	**impose**	**infantry**	**illiterate**	**imperil**

Extend Your Vocabulary

1. Make a list of words with the *im-* or *in-* prefix.
2. Write an expository piece about some ways to help someone who is illiterate.
3. Choose a partner and make a list of words that are synonyms of the word *immense.*
4. Research a ruler who "imposed" his or her views on people. Write a report. Do you think he or she was a successful ruler?

Name: _____   Date: _____

Unit 9: "I" Words: *Vocabulary Quiz*

Directions: Match each vocabulary word with the correct meaning. Write the word on the line next to the meaning.

instantaneous	**impose**	**indelible**	**infuriate**	**intrigue**
inflammable	**infantry**	**immense**	**illustrious**	**impertinent**
indispensable	**inevitable**	**illiterate**	**immaterial**	**imperil**
impudent	**insinuate**	**instigate**	**inclination**	**innumerable**

1. _____ not knowing how to read and write

2. _____ excite the curiosity and interest of

3. _____ urge on; stir up

4. _____ coming or done in an instant

5. _____ absolutely necessary

6. _____ very large; huge; vast

7. _____ not to be avoided; sure to happen

8. _____ fill with wild, fierce anger; make furious

9. _____ suggest in an indirect way

10. _____ not able to be erased or removed

11. _____ natural bent; tendency

12. _____ very famous; great; outstanding

13. _____ cannot be counted; very numerous

14. _____ not pertinent; not to the point; out of place

15. _____ not important; insignificant

16. _____ easily excited or aroused; excitable

17. _____ shamelessly bold; very rude

18. _____ soldiers trained, equipped, and organized to fight on foot

19. _____ put in danger

20. _____ force or thrust one's authority or influence on another

Name: _____   Date: _____

Unit 10: "J" Words: *Vocabulary List and Alphabetizing*

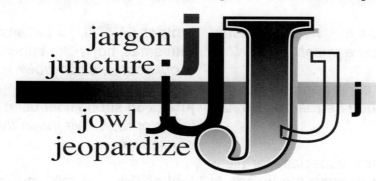

jargon
juncture
jowl
jeopardize

jest (jest)   jubilant (jōō´ bə lənt)

jaunt (jônt)   jovial (jō´ vē əl)

jeopardize (jep´ ər dīz)   jurisdiction (jŏŏr´ is dik´ shən)

joist (joist)   jonquil (jong´ kwəl)

jostle (jos´ əl)   juncture (jungk´ chər)

juniper (jōō´ ni pər)   jute (jōōt)

jabber (jab´ ər)   jalopy (jə lop´ ē)

jargon (jär´ gən)   javelin (jav´ ə lin)

jinx (jingks)   jocular (jok´ yə lər)

journalist (jûr´ nəl ist)   jowl (jowl)

Directions: Write the above vocabulary words in alphabetical order below.

1. _____   11. _____

2. _____   12. _____

3. _____   13. _____

4. _____   14. _____

5. _____   15. _____

6. _____   16. _____

7. _____   17. _____

8. _____   18. _____

9. _____   19. _____

10. _____   20. _____

Unit 10: "J" Words: *Get the Facts!*

jest (jest) poke fun; make fun. *When we jested about his idea, he became upset.*

jubilant (joo´ bə lənt) expressing or showing joy. *He was jubilant when he realized he had won the race.*

jaunt (jônt) short journey, especially for pleasure. *We took a jaunt through the woods to find mushrooms.*

jovial (jō´ vē əl) good-hearted and full of fun; good-humored and merry. *The teacher we have this year is jovial and makes learning a fun experience.*

jeopardize (jep´ ər dīz) put in danger; risk; endanger. *The car pileup jeopardized many lives.*

jurisdiction (joor´ is dik´ shən) right or power to give out justice. *A boss has jurisdiction over his employees.*

joist (joist) one of the parallel beams of timber or steel that supports the boards of a floor or ceiling. *We could hear the joists squeak above us as he walked in the attic.*

jonquil (jong´ kwəl) plant with yellow or white flowers and long, slender leaves. *A jonquil looks similar to a daffodil.*

jostle (jos´ əl) shove, push or crowd against. *We were jostled as we left the crowded arena.*

juncture (jungk´ chər) junction; point or line where two things join. *We were close to the juncture when we realized we had taken a wrong turn.*

juniper (joo´ ni pər) evergreen shrub or tree with small, berry-like cones. *The juniper bush in our front yard has grown much taller this year.*

jute (joot) strong fiber used for making coarse fabric or rope. *We made the plant hanger out of jute rope.*

jabber (jab´ ər) talk very fast in a confused, senseless way. *The toddler's jabber was difficult to understand.*

jalopy (jə lop´ ē) an old automobile in bad condition. *The jalopy was unable to get us to our destination.*

jargon (jär´ gən) language of a special group or profession. *Doctors use a special jargon when they speak of medical procedures.*

javelin (jav´ ə lin) lightweight spear thrown by hand. *He threw the javelin the longest distance in the Olympic competition.*

jinx (jingks) person or thing believed to bring bad luck. *She believed the small statue was a jinx and the cause of all her problems.*

jocular (jok´ yə lər) funny; joking. *The jocular speaker made his audience laugh.*

journalist (jûr´ nəl ist) person whose work is writing for, editing, managing, or publishing a newspaper or magazine. *The journalist had to meet her editor's deadline.*

jowl (jowl) jaw, especially the lower jaw. *The pain in her jowl needed a doctor's attention.*

Name: _____ Date: _____

Unit 10: "J" Words: *Skills and Practice*

Directions: Write a **synonym** from the list of vocabulary words below on the line. A **synonym** is a word that means the same or nearly the same.

jeopardize	**jaunt**	**jowl**	**jonquil**	**juncture**
javelin	**jubilant**	**jest**	**jalopy**	**jabber**

1. excursion _____
2. joint _____
3. joke _____
4. imperil _____
5. car _____
6. rejoicing _____
7. chatter _____
8. daffodil _____
9. jaw _____
10. spear _____

> **Did You Know?** The javelin throw started in the original Olympic Games in ancient Greece and is still one of the Olympic sports today.

Directions: Write an **antonym** from the list of vocabulary words below on the line. An **antonym** is a word that means the opposite or nearly opposite.

jinx	**jocular**	**jovial**

1. wicked _____
2. four-leaf clover _____
3. serious _____

Directions: Write a sentence for each of the vocabulary words below on your own paper. Remember to check your spelling and punctuation.

jurisdiction	**juniper**	**joist**	**jostle**	**jute**
journalist	**jargon**			

Extend Your Vocabulary

1. Write a list of words considered as the jargon of a certain profession.
2. Write a persuasive piece on why students should not jeopardize their futures with drugs and alcohol.
3. Interview a local journalist about his or her job. Share the information with your class.
4. Write a narrative piece about a time when your parents used their jurisdiction over you. Include your feelings and why you felt the way you did.

Name: _____ Date: _____

Unit 10: "J" Words: *Vocabulary Quiz*

Directions: Match each vocabulary word with the correct meaning. Write the word on the line next to the meaning.

jest	jubilant	jaunt	jovial	jeopardize
joist	jonquil	jostle	juncture	jurisdiction
jute	jabber	jalopy	jargon	journalist
jinx	jocular	jowl	javelin	juniper

1. _____ old automobile in bad condition

2. _____ put in danger; risk; endanger

3. _____ person or thing believed to bring bad luck

4. _____ shove, push, or crowd against

5. _____ talk very fast in a confused, senseless way

6. _____ poke fun; make fun

7. _____ language of a special group or profession

8. _____ a short journey, especially for pleasure

9. _____ funny; joking

10. _____ one of the parallel beams of timber or steel that supports the boards of a floor or ceiling

11. _____ jaw, especially the lower jaw

12. _____ junction; point or line where two things join

13. _____ lightweight spear thrown by hand

14. _____ good-hearted and full of fun; good-humored and merry

15. _____ person whose work is writing for, editing, managing, or publishing a newspaper or magazine

16. _____ expressing or showing joy

17. _____ plant with yellow or white flowers and long slender leaves

18. _____ strong fiber used for making coarse fabric or rope

19. _____ right or power to give out justice

20. _____ evergreen shrub or tree with small, berry-like cones

Name: _____ Date: _____

Unit 11: "K" Words: *Vocabulary List and Alphabetizing*

keel (kēl)   khaki (kak´ ē)

knoll (nōl)   kelp (kelp)

kilohertz (kil´ ō herts´)   kilowatt (kil´ ō wot´)

knave (nāv)   kookaburra (kook´ ə bûr´ ə)

kumquat (kum´ kwot)   kudos (koo´ dōs)

krill (kril)   knell (nel)

kale (kāl)   kiosk (kē´ osk´)

kinesthetic (kin´ is thet´ ik)   kibitzer (kib´ it sər)

keen (kēn)   kindhearted (kind´ härt´ id)

kaolin (kā´ ə lin)   kleptomania (klep´ tō mā´ nē ə)

Directions: Write the above vocabulary words in alphabetical order below.

1. _____   11. _____

2. _____   12. _____

3. _____   13. _____

4. _____   14. _____

5. _____   15. _____

6. _____   16. _____

7. _____   17. _____

8. _____   18. _____

9. _____   19. _____

10. _____   20. _____

Unit 11: "K" Words: *Get the Facts!*

keel (kēl) main timber or steel piece that extends the whole length of the bottom of a ship or boat. *A ship is built upon a keel.*

khaki (kak´ ē) dull, yellowish-brown color. *He spilled milk on his khaki pants.*

knoll (nōl) small, round hill. *The prairie dog was perched on the knoll.*

kelp (kelp) large, tough, brown seaweed. *Her fishing hook became entangled in the kelp.*

kilohertz (kil´ ō herts´) 1,000 hertz, used to express the frequency of radio waves. *We learned about kilohertz on our field trip to the radio station.*

kilowatt (kil´ ō wot´) unit of electrical power equal to 1,000 watts. *The voltage was equal to ten kilowatts.*

knave (nāv) tricky, dishonest person; rogue. *Steve, acting like a knave, tricked us into believing his story.*

kookaburra (kook´ ə bûr´ ə) large kingfisher of Australia with a harsh, crackling voice. *The kookaburra is a type of bird in Australia.*

kumquat (kum´ kwot) a yellow or orange fruit, somewhat like a small orange. *We used kumquats in our preserves.*

kudos (koo´ dōs) glory; fame. *The teacher replied, "Kudos for you," when the child answered the question correctly.*

krill (kril) a small, shrimp-like shellfish that is eaten by whales and other sea animals. *Krill are a main part of a puffin's diet.*

knell (nel) sound of a bell rung slowly after a death or at a funeral. *The knell of the bells was a sad sound for the bereaved family.*

kleptomania (klep´ tō mā´ nē ə) abnormal, irresistible desire to steal, especially things that one does not need. *She suffers from kleptomania and has been arrested for shoplifting.*

kiosk (kē´ osk´) a small building with one or more sides open, used as a newsstand, a bandstand, or an opening to a subway. *She stopped at the kiosk in the subway to buy a magazine.*

kinesthetic (kin´ is thet´ ik) having to do with sensations of motion from the muscles and joints. *He was a better kinesthetic learner than a verbal learner.*

kibitzer (kib´ it sər) person who gives unwanted advice. *She was a kibitzer and constantly wanted to interfere in our lives.*

keen (kēn) sharp; cutting. *The keen pain from his broken ankle slowed us down.*

kindhearted (kind´ härt´ id) having or showing a kind heart; kindly. *The kindhearted man offered us a ride.*

kaolin (kā´ ə lin) fine white clay used in making porcelain. *The girl needed more kaolin to finish her vase in art class.*

kale (kāl) kind of cabbage that has loose, curled leaves that are eaten as a vegetable. *The vegetable stand was selling kale and tomatoes, along with many other fresh vegetables.*

Name: _____ Date: _____

Unit 11: "K" Words: *Skills and Practice*

Directions: Write a **synonym** from the list of vocabulary words below on the line. A **synonym** is a word that means the same or nearly the same.

| kindhearted | knave | keen | knoll | kudos |
| kibitzer | khaki | kelp | | |

1. seaweed _____   2. rascal _____
3. tan _____   4. sharp _____
5. meddler _____   6. mound _____
7. praise _____   8. sympathetic _____

> **Did You Know?** *Kilo* means "one thousand." The prefix *kilo-* is from French *kilo,* which came from Greek *chilioi.*

Directions: Match the noun with the correct vocabulary word.

| kumquat | kale | kookaburra | krill | kaolin | knell |

1. bird _____   2. fruit _____
3. shellfish _____   4. bell _____
5. clay _____   6. cabbage _____

Directions: Write a sentence for each of the vocabulary words below on your own paper. Remember to check your spelling and punctuation.

| kleptomania | kilohertz | keel | kilowatt | kiosk |
| kinesthetic | | | | |

Extend Your Vocabulary

1. Design a food chain using krill as one of the links.
2. Make a list of animals unique to Australia, such as the kookaburra.
3. Create a word map of the different shades of brown, including khaki.
4. Research the different learning styles, including kinesthetic learning. Write a report.

Name: _____ Date: _____

Unit 11: "K" Words: *Vocabulary Quiz*

Directions: Match each vocabulary word with the correct meaning. Write the word on the line next to the meaning.

kilohertz	**keel**	**khaki**	**knoll**	**kinesthetic**
kilowatt	**kelp**	**knave**	**kudos**	**kookaburra**
kumquat	**krill**	**knell**	**kiosk**	**kleptomania**
kibitzer	**keen**	**kaolin**	**kale**	**kindhearted**

1. _____ small building with one or more sides open, used as a newsstand, a bandstand, or an opening to a subway

2. _____ dull, yellowish-brown color

3. _____ person who gives unwanted advice

4. _____ unit of electrical power equal to 1,000 watts

5. _____ fine, white clay used in making porcelain

6. _____ a large kingfisher of Australia with a harsh, crackling voice

7. _____ abnormal, irresistible desire to steal, especially things that one does not need

8. _____ main timber or steel piece that extends the whole length of the bottom of a ship or boat

9. _____ sharp; cutting

10. _____ sound of a bell rung slowly after a death or at a funeral

11. _____ kind of cabbage that has loose, curled leaves that are eaten as a vegetable

12. _____ small, round hill

13. _____ having to do with sensations of motion from the muscles and joints

14. _____ 1,000 hertz, used to express the frequency of radio waves

15. _____ having or showing a kind heart; kindly

16. _____ yellow or orange fruit somewhat like a small orange

17. _____ large, tough, brown seaweed

18. _____ glory; fame

19. _____ tricky, dishonest person; rogue

20. _____ small, shrimp-like shellfish that is eaten by whales and other sea animals

44

Name: _____   Date: _____

Unit 12: "L" Words: *Vocabulary List and Alphabetizing*

lacquer (lak´ ər)

laden (lād´ ən)

lavatory (lav´ ə tôr ē)

lunatic (lōō´ nə tik)

laborious (lə bôr´ ē əs)

listless (list´ lis)

lenient (lēn´ yənt)

larceny (lär´ sə nē)

loathe (lōth)

lanky (langk´ ē)

lope (lōp)

lance (lans)

lichen (lī´ kən)

liberate (lib´ ə rāt)

lucid (lōō´ sid)

lurk (lûrk)

lynch (linch)

lax (laks)

lacerate (las´ ə rāt)

languish (lang´ gwish)

Directions: Write the above vocabulary words in alphabetical order below.

1. _____   11. _____

2. _____   12. _____

3. _____   13. _____

4. _____   14. _____

5. _____   15. _____

6. _____   16. _____

7. _____   17. _____

8. _____   18. _____

9. _____   19. _____

10. _____   20. _____

45

Unit 12: "L" Words: *Get the Facts!*

lacquer (lak´ ər) varnish used to give a protective coating or a shiny appearance to metal or wood. *The painter put lacquer on the bench in the yard to protect it from the weather.*

lope (lōp) to run with a long, easy stride. *The gazelle loped across the plains.*

laden (lād´ ən) loaded. *The mules were laden with tools for the miner.*

lance (lans) long wooden spear with a sharp iron or steel head. *The knight's lance broke during the jousting tournament.*

lavatory (lav´ ə tôr ē) bowl or basin to wash in; toilet. *After the long trip, the children needed to use the lavatory.*

lichen (lī´ kən) flowerless plant that looks somewhat like moss and consists of a fungus and an algae growing together as one plant. *The lichen was growing on the mountainside.*

lunatic (loo´ nə tik) insane; extremely foolish. *The lunatic man thought he was a dog.*

liberate (lib´ ə rāt) set free. *The prisoners were liberated by the Allies.*

laborious (lə bôr´ ē əs) requiring hard work; industrious. *The painter worked six days a week at the laborious task of restoring the statues in the church.*

lucid (loo´ sid) clear; transparent. *The lucid water was a beautiful sight to the hiker.*

listless (list´ lis) seeming too tired to care about anything; not interested in things; not caring to be active. *The sick child was listless and couldn't be tempted by either food or toys.*

lurk (lûrk) to stay hidden, ready to spring out or attack; to exist undiscovered or unobserved. *The cat lurked in the tall grass waiting for the mouse to appear.*

lenient (lēn´ yənt) mild or gentle; not harsh or stern. *The lenient judge gave the first offender probation instead of a prison sentence.*

lynch (linch) put an accused person to death, usually by hanging, without a lawful trial. *In the Old West, cattle rustlers were often lynched.*

larceny (lär´ sə nē) the unlawful taking and using of the personal property of another person. *The woman was put in jail for larceny.*

lax (laks) not firm or tight; slack. *The lax rope caused the acrobat to fall to the ground.*

loathe (lōth) feel strong dislike and disgust; intense aversion. *She loathes any type of spider.*

lacerate (las´ ə rāt) tear roughly. *The skin on the child's forehead was lacerated by the sharp corner of the table.*

lanky (langk´ ē) long and thin; slender. *The lanky boy's height allowed him to excel at basketball.*

languish (lang´ gwish) grow weak; become weary; lose energy. *The woman languished during her long illness.*

Name: _____ Date: _____

Unit 12: "L" Words: *Skills and Practice*

Directions: Write a **synonym** from the list of vocabulary words below on the line. A **synonym** is a word that means the same or nearly the same.

lacquer	**lacerate**	**laden**	**lance**	**lunatic**
lavatory	**larceny**	**lurk**		

1. burdened _____

2. idiotic _____

3. spear _____

4. sneak _____

5. theft _____

6. varnish _____

7. bathroom _____

8. mangle _____

Did You Know? *Larceny* came into the English language about 600 years ago from French *larcin* and can be traced back to Latin, meaning "a bandit or hired soldier."

Directions: Write an **antonym** from the list of vocabulary words below on the line. An **antonym** is a word that means the opposite or nearly opposite.

lenient	**lucid**	**lanky**	**laborious**	**liberate**
listless	**loathe**	**lax**		

1. dull _____

2. capture _____

3. active _____

4. harsh _____

5. lazy _____

6. tight _____

7. love _____

8. broad _____

Directions: Write a sentence for each of the vocabulary words below on your own paper. Remember to check your spelling and punctuation.

lichen	**lope**	**lynch**	**languish**

Extend Your Vocabulary

1. Make a list of various words that mean "run," such as *lope.*
2. Write about something you loathe. Give numerous reasons why.
3. Pretend you are a prisoner of war. Name the war, describe the conditions, and tell how you felt about being liberated.
4. Research the plant lichen. In what biome would you find it? Write a report.

Name: _____ Date: _____

Unit 12: "L" Words: *Vocabulary Quiz*

Directions: Match each vocabulary word with the correct meaning. Write the word on the line next to the meaning.

lacquer	**lope**	**laden**	**lance**	**lavatory**
lichen	**lurk**	**lanky**	**lucid**	**liberate**
larceny	**lax**	**lynch**	**laborious**	**lunatic**
listless	**loathe**	**lenient**	**lacerate**	**languish**

1. _____ mild or gentle; not harsh or stern

2. _____ to run with a long, easy stride

3. _____ to stay hidden, ready to spring out or attack; to exist undiscovered or unobserved

4. _____ bowl or basin to wash in; toilet

5. _____ feel strong dislike and disgust; intense aversion

6. _____ set free

7. _____ put an accused person to death, usually by hanging, without a lawful trial

8. _____ varnish used to give a protective coating or a shiny appearance to metal or wood

9. _____ tear roughly

10. _____ clear; transparent

11. _____ unlawful taking and using of the personal property of another person

12. _____ long, wooden spear with a sharp iron or steel head

13. _____ long and thin; slender

14. _____ insane; extremely foolish

15. _____ grow weak; become weary; lose energy

16. _____ flowerless plant that looks somewhat like moss and consists of a fungus and an algae growing together as one plant

17. _____ not firm or tight; slack

18. _____ loaded

19. _____ requiring hard work; industrious

20. _____ seeming too tired to care about anything; not interested in things; not caring to be active

Name: _____   Date: _____

Unit 13: "M" Words: *Vocabulary List and Alphabetizing*

mishap (mis´ hap)

midst (midst)

mutiny (myo͞ot´ 'n ē)

morose (mə rōs´)

menagerie (mə naj´ ər ē)

misfortune (mis fôr´ chən)

matron (mā´ trən)

magistrate (maj´ is strāt)

misdemeanor (mis´ də mē´ nər)

meander (mē an´ dər)

meddle (med´ əl)

monotonous (mə not´ 'n əs)

maestro (mī´ strō)

menace (men´ is)

misguide (mis gīd´)

misnomer (mis nō´ mər)

molten (mōlt´ 'n)

mastication (mas´ ti kā´ shən)

misanthrope (mis´ ən thrōp)

memorandum (mem´ ə ran´ dəm)

Directions: Write the above vocabulary words in alphabetical order below.

1. _____
2. _____
3. _____
4. _____
5. _____
6. _____
7. _____
8. _____
9. _____
10. _____

11. _____
12. _____
13. _____
14. _____
15. _____
16. _____
17. _____
18. _____
19. _____
20. _____

Unit 13: "M" Words: *Get the Facts!*

mishap (mis´ hap) an unlucky accident. *Her mishap landed her in the hospital.*

meddle (med´ əl) busy oneself with or in other people's affairs without being asked or needed. *Our nosy neighbor always tries to meddle in my business.*

midst (midst) the middle part. *Tammy was in the midst of taking a test when she got a headache.*

monotonous (mə not´ 'n əs) continuing in the same tone; without change. *The monotonous voice of the professor made us want to sleep through class.*

mutiny (myo͞ot´ 'n ē) open rebellion against lawful authority, especially by sailors or soldiers against their officers. *The mutiny of the angry sailors turned violent.*

maestro (mī´ strō) great composer, teacher, or conductor of music. *The maestro began the concert when we were all seated.*

morose (mə rōs´) gloomy, ill-humored; sullen. *A morose person's mood can affect everyone around them.*

menace (men´ is) threaten; a threat. *The mean dog was a menace to the people in our neighborhood.*

menagerie (mə naj´ ər ē) collection of wild animals kept in cages for exhibition. *We explored the menagerie on our field trip to the zoo.*

misguide (mis gīd´) lead into mistakes or wrongdoing. *The woman at the door of the museum unintentionally misguided the group.*

misfortune (mis fôr´ chən) bad luck. *It was her misfortune to forget her report.*

misnomer (mis nō´ mər) name that describes wrongly. *Calling the conscientious manager lazy was a misnomer on her part.*

matron (mā´ trən) woman who manages the household matters of a school, hospital, or other institution. *The school matron was in charge of the students.*

molten (mōlt´ 'n) made into liquid by heat. *The molten steel was used in large quantities by the factory.*

magistrate (maj´ is strāt) government official who has the power to apply the law and put it into force. *The magistrate was in charge of the investigation.*

mastication (mas´ ti kā´ shən) act of chewing. *The boy's mastication of gum was loud and disruptive.*

misdemeanor (mis´ də mē´ nər) breaking of the law, not as serious as a felony. *The misdemeanor was put on the boy's record.*

misanthrope (mis´ ən thrōp) person who dislikes or distrusts people in general. *A misanthrope has a difficult time being satisfied and happy.*

meander (mē an´ dər) follow a winding course. *She meandered along the beautiful, flowered path.*

memorandum (mem´ ə ran´ dəm) short, written statement for future use. *Please type a memorandum regarding the agenda for the conference.*

Name: _____ Date: _____

Unit 13: "M" Words: *Skills and Practice*

Directions: Write a **synonym** from the list of vocabulary words below on the line. A **synonym** is a word that means the same or nearly the same.

molten	**mishap**	**magistrate**	**misguide**	**misfortune**
meander	**meddle**	**mastication**	**midst**	**memorandum**

1. trouble _____

2. mislead _____

3. note _____

4. interfere _____

5. leader _____

6. calamity _____

7. middle _____

8. stroll _____

9. chewing _____

10. melted _____

> **Did You Know?** The prefix *mis-* means "bad" or "wrong," as in *mispronunciation*.

Directions: Write an **antonym** from the list of vocabulary words below on the line. An **antonym** is a word that means the opposite or nearly opposite.

misanthrope	**menace**	**mutiny**	**morose**	**monotonous**

1. change _____

2. cheerful _____

3. obedience _____

4. optimist _____

5. console _____

Directions: Write a sentence for each of the vocabulary words below on your own paper. Remember to check your spelling and punctuation.

maestro	**menagerie**	**misnomer**	**matron**	**misdemeanor**

Extend Your Vocabulary

1. Write a narrative piece about a mishap that you experienced or saw happen. Remember to include your reactions and feelings.
2. Make a list of things that can be monotonous. Share and compare with a friend.
3. Research a great maestro and write a report. Include all parts of his or her life and what may have inspired him or her to pursue his or her musical career.
4. Create a list of misdemeanors and the consequences of committing a misdemeanor.

Name: _____ Date: _____

Unit 13: "M" Words: *Vocabulary Quiz*

Directions: Match each vocabulary word with the correct meaning. Write the word on the line next to the meaning.

misnomer	**meddle**	**midst**	**monotonous**	**memorandum**
maestro	**menace**	**matron**	**menagerie**	**misguide**
misfortune	**mishap**	**molten**	**magistrate**	**misanthrope**
mastication	**morose**	**mutiny**	**meander**	**misdemeanor**

1. _____ woman who manages the household matters of a school, hospital, or other institution

2. _____ the middle part

3. _____ act of chewing

4. _____ great composer, teacher, or conductor of music

5. _____ bad luck

6. _____ unlucky accident

7. _____ made into liquid by heat

8. _____ open rebellion against lawful authority, especially by sailors or soldiers against their officers

9. _____ person who dislikes or distrusts people in general

10. _____ threaten; threat

11. _____ name that describes wrongly

12. _____ busy oneself with or in other people's affairs without being asked or needed

13. _____ government official who has power to apply the law and put it in force

14. _____ short, written statement for future use

15. _____ follow a winding course

16. _____ lead into mistakes or wrongdoing

17. _____ gloomy; ill-humored; sullen

18. _____ continuing in the same tone; without change

19. _____ collection of wild animals kept in cages for exhibition

20. _____ breaking of the law, not as serious as a felony

Name: _____ Date: _____

Unit 14: "N" Words: *Vocabulary List and Alphabetizing*

nausea (nô´ zē ə)

novelty (nov´ əl tē)

necessitate (nə ses´ ə tāt´)

nonchalant (non´ shə lont´)

naive (nä ēv´)

negate (ni gāt´)

nonsensical (non sen´ si kəl)

necrosis (ne krō´ sis)

noxious (nok´ shəs)

nuptial (nup´ shəl)

nomad (nō´ mad)

notorious (nō tôr´ ē əs)

neurotic (noō rot´ ik)

notation (nō tā´ shən)

notoriety (nōt´ ə rī´ ə tē)

negligible (neg´ lə jə bəl)

nonpareil (non´ pə rel´)

nostalgia (nəs tal´ jə)

nuance (noō´ ons´)

nonconformist (non´ kən fôr´ mist)

Directions: Write the above vocabulary words in alphabetical order below.

1. _____

2. _____

3. _____

4. _____

5. _____

6. _____

7. _____

8. _____

9. _____

10. _____

11. _____

12. _____

13. _____

14. _____

15. _____

16. _____

17. _____

18. _____

19. _____

20. _____

Unit 14: "N" Words: *Get the Facts!*

nausea (nô´ zē ə) the feeling that one has when about to vomit; extreme disgust. *She felt nauseated after she saw the documentary on television about the clubbing of animals.*

nomad (nō´ mad) wanderer. *He was a nomad his entire life, traveling all over the world.*

novelty (nov´ əl tē) novel character; a new or unusual thing. *The novelty of the child's new toys soon wore off, and he became fretful.*

notorious (nō tôr´ ē əs) well known or commonly known, especially because of something bad. *Al Capone was a notorious gangster.*

necessitate (nə ses´ ə tāt´) make necessary; compel. *His infected gallbladder necessitated an operation.*

neurotic (noo rot´ ik) having or suffering from a neurosis or emotional disorder. *She is neurotic about being in a crowd.*

nonchalant (non´ shə lont´) without enthusiasm; indifferent. *She was nonchalant about the accident.*

notation (nō tā´ shən) note to assist memory; record. *She made a notation to her son about his dentist appointment.*

naive (nä ēv´) simple in nature, like a child; not sophisticated. *He is naive about financial matters, often making bad investments.*

notoriety (nōt´ ə rī´ ə tē) being famous for something bad; ill fame. *The crime brought notoriety to the small town.*

negate (ni gāt´) destroy; make ineffective; deny. *The charges against the woman were negated by her alibi.*

negligible (neg´ lə jə bəl) able to be disregarded. *The loss of her pen was negligible.*

nonsensical (non sen´ si kəl) foolish or absurd. *His nonsensical behavior was observed by all at the party.*

nonpareil (non´ pə rel´) person or thing having no equal. *Michael Jordan is a nonpareil in basketball.*

necrosis (ne krō´ sis) the death or decay of tissue in a particular part of the body. *The severe burn caused necrosis of the skin on his finger.*

nostalgia (nəs tal´ jə) painful yearning for one's home, country, city, or for anything far removed in space or time. *He wished with nostalgia for the music of the '40s to return.*

noxious (nok´ shəs) very harmful; poisonous. *Noxious fumes came from the burning chemical plant.*

nuance (noo´ ons´) slight variation in expression, tone, feeling, or color. *The nuance of fear was seen on her face when she heard the unfamiliar sound outside.*

nuptial (nup´ shəl) of marriage or weddings. *The nuptial ceremony was very beautiful and moving.*

nonconformist (non´ kən fôr´ mist) one who refuses to conform or accept the established laws, rules, or customs of a group. *When a gang is planning to do something illegal or destructive, it is better to be a nonconformist, instead of going along with the group.*

Name: _____   Date: _____

Unit 14: "N" Words: *Skills and Practice*

Directions: Write a **synonym** from the list of vocabulary words below on the line. A **synonym** is a word that means the same or nearly the same.

necrosis	**novelty**	**negate**	**notation**	**notorious**
necessitate	**notoriety**	**nausea**		

1. well known _____   2. jotting _____
3. loathing _____   4. nullify _____
5. ill fame _____   6. newness _____
7. force _____   8. decay _____

> **Did You Know?** There are many prefixes that express negation in the English language. Some prefixes that mean "not" include *a-* as in *apathy, an-* as in *anorexia, ir-* as in *irregular, neg-* as in *negative,* and *non-* as in *nondescript.*

Directions: Write an **antonym** from the list of vocabulary words below on the line. An **antonym** is a word that means the opposite or nearly opposite.

negligible	**nomad**	**noxious**	**nonsensical**	**nonconformist**
nonchalant	**naive**			

1. settler _____   2. conformer _____
3. nonpoisonous _____   4. concerned _____
5. worldly-wise _____   6. wise _____
7. noticeable _____

Directions: Write a sentence for each of the vocabulary words below on your own paper. Remember to check your spelling and punctuation.

necessitate	**nonpareil**	**nostalgia**	**nuance**	**nuptial**

Extend Your Vocabulary

1. Research the nomadic tribes of Africa. Write a report about their lifestyles.
2. Compare and contrast the nuptial ceremonies of two different countries. Use a T-chart or Venn diagram.
3. List several people who are notorious and the reasons for their bad reputations.
4. List as many novelties as you can that are "in" right now. One example would be yo-yo's.

Name: _____ Date: _____

Unit 14: "N" Words: *Vocabulary Quiz*

Directions: Match each vocabulary word with the correct meaning. Write the word on the line next to the meaning.

nausea	nomad	novelty	nuance	necessitate
neurotic	naive	nonchalant	notation	necrosis
notoriety	negate	negligible	nonpareil	nonsensical
nostalgia	noxious	notorious	nuptial	nonconformist

1. _____ person or thing having no equal

2. _____ well known or commonly known, especially because of something bad

3. _____ able to be disregarded

4. _____ having or suffering from a neurosis or emotional disorder

5. _____ slight variation in expression, tone, feeling, or color

6. _____ simple in nature, like a child; not sophisticated

7. _____ foolish or absurd

8. _____ the feeling that one has when about to vomit; extreme disgust

9. _____ one who refuses to conform or accept the established laws, rules, or customs of a group

10. _____ wanderer

11. _____ the death or decay of tissue in a particular part of the body

12. _____ make necessary; compel

13. _____ very harmful; poisonous

14. _____ without enthusiasm; indifferent

15. _____ painful yearning for one's home, country, city, or for anything far removed in space or time

16. _____ note to assist memory; record

17. _____ of marriage or weddings

18. _____ destroy; make ineffective; deny

19. _____ novel character; a new or unusual thing

20. _____ being famous for something bad; ill fame

Name: _____ Date: _____

Unit 15: "O" Words: *Vocabulary List and Alphabetizing*

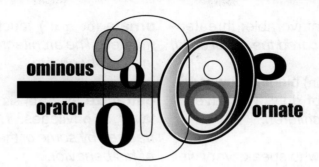

ominous (om´ ə nəs)

orator (ôr´ ət ər)

ordinance (ôrd´ 'n əns)

obsolete (ob´ sə lēt´)

oblique (ō blēk´)

onslaught (ôn´ slôt´)

ostracize (os´ trə sīz´)

oblivion (ə bliv´ ē ən)

oppress (ə pres´)

orifice (ôr´ ə fis)

obligation (ob´ li gā´ shən)

originate (ə rij´ i nāt´)

overture (ō´ vər chər)

optimistic (op´ tə mis´ tik)

obscure (ob skyo͝or´)

ornate (ôr nāt´)

obdurate (ob´ do͝or it)

onerous (on´ ər əs)

opulent (op´ yo͞o lənt)

ornery (ôr´ nər ē)

Directions: Write the above vocabulary words in alphabetical order below.

1. _____

2. _____

3. _____

4. _____

5. _____

6. _____

7. _____

8. _____

9. _____

10. _____

11. _____

12. _____

13. _____

14. _____

15. _____

16. _____

17. _____

18. _____

19. _____

20. _____

Unit 15 "O" Words: *Get the Facts!*

ominous (om´ ə nəs) unfavorable; threatening. *His ominous words scared the small child.*

obligation (ob´ li gā´ shən) binding power of a law, promise, or sense of duty. *We have an obligation to protect our children.*

orator (ôr´ ət ər) person who speaks very well in public. *The Greek orators gave long speeches to the public.*

originate (ə rij´ i nāt´) invent; begin; arise. *Where did pizza originate?*

ordinance (ôrd´ 'n əns) established rule, rite, or law. *Allowing your pet to run loose is a violation of a city ordinance.*

overture (ō´ vər chər) proposal or offer; musical composition played at the beginning of an opera or symphony. *The two warring countries made overtures for peace.*

obsolete (ob´ sə lēt´) no longer in use; out of date. *The typewriter is quickly becoming obsolete with the wide use of computers.*

optimistic (op´ tə mis´ tik) looks on the bright side of things. *She has always been an optimistic person, which helped during her illness.*

oblique (ō blēk´) not straightforward. *He made an oblique response to the question.*

obscure (ob skyŏor´) not clearly expressed; hard to understand; vague. *That passage in the book is obscure.*

onslaught (ôn´ slôt´) vigorous attack. *The country's people had difficulty recovering from the onslaught of their enemies.*

ornate (ôr nāt´) much adorned, much ornamented. *The architectural trim on the old building is very ornate.*

ostracize (os´ trə sīz´) shut out from society, favor, or privileges. *The new student was ostracized by some of the other students because of his behavior.*

obdurate (ob´ dŏor it) stubborn or unyielding. *The obdurate mule refused to move out of the car's path.*

oblivion (ə bliv´ ē ən) condition of being entirely forgotten. *Many ancient customs have disappeared into oblivion.*

onerous (on´ ər əs) hard to carry or take. *The young boy found the heavy package too onerous to carry.*

oppress (ə pres´) govern harshly; keep down unjustly or by cruelty. *The oppressed people of the country rebelled against their cruel leader.*

opulent (op´ yŏo lənt) having wealth; rich. *In the king's palace the furnishings were opulent.*

orifice (ôr´ ə fis) opening or hole; mouth. *The rock climbers could not see into the dark orifice of the cave.*

ornery (ôr´ nər ē) mean in disposition. *The ornery dog was not a good pet.*

Name: _____ Date: _____

Unit 15 "O" Words: *Skills and Practice*

Directions: Write a **synonym** from the list of vocabulary words below on the line. A **synonym** is a word that means the same or nearly the same.

onslaught	obligation	overture	orator	oblique
obsolete	onerous	obdurate		

1. burdensome _____
2. indirect _____
3. offer _____
4. speaker _____
5. old-fashioned _____
6. assault _____
7. duty _____
8. obstinate _____

Did You Know? *Overture* came into the English language about 600 years ago from French *overture,* which came from Latin, meaning "opening."

Directions: Write an **antonym** from the list of vocabulary words below on the line. An **antonym** is a word that means the opposite or nearly opposite.

opulent	ornate	ominous	ostracize	optimistic
obscure	ornery	originate	obdurate	

1. flexible _____
2. pessimistic _____
3. favorable _____
4. kind _____
5. clear _____
6. accept _____
7. end _____
8. poor _____
9. plain _____

Directions: Write a sentence for each of the vocabulary words below on your own paper. Remember to check your spelling and punctuation.

oblivion	ordinance	oppress	orifice

Extend Your Vocabulary

1. List as many words as you can that have multiple meanings, such as *overture.*
2. Research your last name. Where did it originate? What does it mean? Write a mini-report.
3. Write a report on one great orator (Greek, Roman, etc.).
4. Write about an obligation you have with your family. How does it make you feel?

Name: _____ Date: _____

Unit 15: "O" Words: *Vocabulary Quiz*

Directions: Match each vocabulary word with the correct meaning. Write the word on the line next to the meaning.

ominous	**obligation**	**orator**	**originate**	**ordinance**
overture	**obsolete**	**optimistic**	**oblique**	**obscure**
onslaught	**ostracize**	**obdurate**	**oblivion**	**onerous**
oppress	**opulent**	**orifice**	**ornery**	**ornate**

1. _____ condition of being entirely forgotten

2. _____ unfavorable; threatening

3. _____ shut out from society, favor, or privileges

4. _____ invent; begin; arise

5. _____ govern harshly; keep down unjustly or by cruelty

6. _____ looks on the bright side of things

7. _____ opening or hole; mouth

8. _____ not clearly expressed; hard to understand; vague

9. _____ mean in disposition

10. _____ established rule, rite, or law

11. _____ stubborn or unyielding

12. _____ binding power of a law, promise, or sense of duty

13. _____ hard to carry or take

14. _____ person who speaks very well in public

15. _____ having wealth; rich

16. _____ no longer in use; out of date

17. _____ not straight-forward

18. _____ vigorous attack

19. _____ proposal or offer; musical composition played at the beginning of an opera or symphony

20. _____ much adorned; much ornamented

Name: _____ Date: _____

Unit 16: "P" Words: *Vocabulary List and Alphabetizing*

preside

prelude

privy

predicament (prē dik´ ə mənt)

propaganda (prop´ ə gan´ də)

predominant (prē dom´ ə nənt)

provision (prə vizh´ ən)

premonition (prem´ ə nish´ ən)

pugnacious (pug nā´ shəs)

postulate (pos´ chə lāt´)

pretentious (prē ten´ shəs)

peripatetic (per´ i pə tet´ ik)

privy (priv´ ē)

preside (prē zīd´)

prosperous (pros´ pər əs)

propulsion (prə pul´ shən)

prelude (prā´ lood)

preposterous (prē pos´ tər əs)

periodical (pir´ ē od´ i kəl)

predatory (pred´ ə tôr´ ē)

profound (prō found´)

posthumous (pos´ choo məs)

punctilious (pungk til´ ē əs)

Directions: Write the above vocabulary words in alphabetical order below.

1. _____ 11. _____

2. _____ 12. _____

3. _____ 13. _____

4. _____ 14. _____

5. _____ 15. _____

6. _____ 16. _____

7. _____ 17. _____

8. _____ 18. _____

9. _____ 19. _____

10. _____ 20. _____

Unit 16: "P" Words: *Get the Facts!*

predicament (prē dik´ ə mənt) unpleasant, difficult, or bad situation. *She was in a predicament when she lost her car keys.*

preside (prē zīd´) hold the place of authority; have control. *The chairman presides at the stockholders' meeting.*

propaganda (prop´ ə gan´ də) systematic efforts to spread opinions or beliefs; any plan or method for spreading opinions or beliefs. *Propaganda can cause destruction when people are not knowledgeable about the facts.*

prosperous (pros´ pər əs) doing well; successful; fortunate. *Mr. Martin's store is prosperous because he always treats his customers well.*

predominant (prē dom´ ə nənt) most noticeable. *Yellow is the predominant color in her house.*

propulsion (prə pul´ shən) propelling force or impulse; driving forward or onward. *The propulsion of the motor powered the speedboat.*

provision (prə vizh´ ən) act of providing; something provided or prepared for the future. *There is a provision for their children in their will.*

prelude (prā´ lōōd) anything serving as an introduction. *Her speech was a prelude to the play.*

premonition (prem´ ə nish´ ən) forewarning. *She had a premonition that something terrible was going to happen.*

preposterous (prē pos´ tər əs) contrary to reason; absurd; senseless; foolish. *It is preposterous to go to the office in a bathing suit on hot days.*

pugnacious (pug nā´ shəs) having the habit of fighting; quarrelsome. *His pugnacious personality gets him into trouble at school.*

periodical (pir´ ē od´ i kəl) magazine that appears regularly; published at regular intervals, often less than daily. <u>Newsweek</u> *is a periodical.*

postulate (pos´ chə lāt´) assume without proof; take for granted; require; demand. *The spectators in the courtroom postulated that the man was guilty before the testimony was presented.*

predatory (pred´ ə tôr´ ē) living by preying upon other animals. *Alligators are predatory animals.*

pretentious (prē ten´ shəs) making claims to excellence or importance. *The pretentious actress always traveled in a limousine.*

profound (prō found´) very deep; deeply felt; very great; having or showing great knowledge. *He made a profound speech about losing a loved one.*

peripatetic (per´ i pə tet´ ik) walking about; traveling from place to place. *The salesman was a peripatetic person, selling his products all over the state.*

posthumous (pos´ chōō məs) happening after death. *The firefighter received a posthumous honor for his rescue of the child at the cost of his own life.*

privy (priv´ ē) private. *He was privy to the information about the bank's security system.*

punctilious (pungk til´ ē əs) very careful and exact. *The accountant was punctilious about his bookkeeping figures.*

Name: _____   Date: _____

Unit 16: "P" Words: *Skills and Practice*

Directions: Write a **synonym** from the list of vocabulary words below on the line. A **synonym** is a word that means the same or nearly the same.

prosperous	predominant	prelude	profound	predicament
provision	periodical	postulate	premonition	

1. introduction _____   2. thriving _____
3. claim _____   4. prevailing _____
5. great _____   6. preparation _____
7. magazine _____   8. dilemma _____
9. forewarning _____

Did You Know? The prefix *pre-* means "before," as in *prewar*. The prefix *post-* means "after in time" or "later," as in *postscript*.

Directions: Write an **antonym** from the list of vocabulary words below on the line. An **antonym** is a word that means the opposite or nearly opposite.

predatory	punctilious	privy	preposterous	pretentious
peripatetic	pugnacious			

1. logical _____   2. prey _____
3. public _____   4. humble _____
5. peaceable _____   6. inaccurate _____
7. homebody _____

Directions: Write a sentence for each of the vocabulary words below on your own paper. Remember to check your spelling and punctuation.

preside	propaganda	propulsion	posthumous

Extend Your Vocabulary

1. Watch a sample of television commercials. Notice the propaganda techniques used. Give examples.
2. Tell a preposterous story to a friend.
3. Make a list of periodicals.
4. Write a persuasive piece about why you think someone is prosperous, but not necessarily wealthy.

63

Name: _____   Date: _____

Unit 16: "P" Words: *Vocabulary Quiz*

Directions: Match each vocabulary word with the correct meaning. Write the word on the line next to the meaning.

predicament	**preside**	**propaganda**	**prosperous**	**postulate**
propulsion	**prelude**	**provision**	**premonition**	**periodical**
preposterous	**privy**	**predatory**	**pretentious**	**pugnacious**
predominant	**profound**	**peripatetic**	**posthumous**	**punctilious**

1. _____ magazine that appears regularly; published at regular intervals, often less than daily

2. _____ systematic efforts to spread opinions or beliefs; any plan or method for spreading opinions or beliefs

3. _____ making claims to excellence or importance

4. _____ most noticeable

5. _____ having the habit of fighting; quarrelsome

6. _____ an unpleasant, difficult, or bad situation

7. _____ very deep; deeply felt; very great; having or showing great knowledge

8. _____ act of providing; something provided or prepared for the future

9. _____ assume without proof; take for granted; require; demand

10. _____ hold the place of authority; have control

11. _____ walking about; traveling from place to place

12. _____ anything serving as an introduction

13. _____ very careful and exact

14. _____ contrary to reason; absurd; senseless; foolish

15. _____ living by preying on other animals

16. _____ doing well; successful; fortunate

17. _____ happening after death

18. _____ forewarning

19. _____ private

20. _____ propelling force or impulse; a driving forward or onward

Name: _____   Date: _____

Unit 17: "Q" Words: *Vocabulary List and Alphabetizing*

quadruple (kwo droo´ pəl)   questionnaire (kwes´ chə ner´)

query (kwir´ ē)   quota (kwō´ tə)

qualm (kwom)   quadratic (kwo drat´ ik)

quaint (kwānt)   quandary (kwon´ dər ē)

quatrain (kwo´ trān)   quell (kwel)

quirk (kwerk)   quorum (kwôr´ əm)

quoin (koin)   quittance (kwit´ 'ns)

quisling (kwiz´ ling)   quirt (kwert)

quiescent (kwē es´ ənt)   queue (kū)

querulous (kwer´ ū ləs)   queasy (kwē´ zē)

Directions: Write the above vocabulary words in alphabetical order below.

1. _____   11. _____

2. _____   12. _____

3. _____   13. _____

4. _____   14. _____

5. _____   15. _____

6. _____   16. _____

7. _____   17. _____

8. _____   18. _____

9. _____   19. _____

10. _____   20. _____

Unit 17: "Q" Words: *Get the Facts*

quadruple (kwo droo´ pəl) consisting of four parts; including four parts or parties; four times. *The four men entered a quadruple agreement.*

questionnaire (kwes´ chə ner´) written or printed list of questions used to gather information or to obtain a sampling of opinions. *A questionnaire was sent to my house concerning my opinion of various television programs.*

query (kwir´ ē) question; inquiry. *She had a query about the proper use of seat belts.*

quota (kwō´ tə) share of the total due from or to a particular district, state, or person. *Each member of the band had a quota of candy to sell.*

qualm (kwom) sudden disturbing feeling in the mind; uneasiness; misgiving. *She tried the strange food despite having a few qualms.*

quadratic (kwo drat´ ik) of or like a square. *In algebra class, we learned about quadratic equations.*

quaint (kwānt) strange or odd in an interesting, pleasing, or amusing way. *The elderly lady's elaborately decorated hat was quaint.*

quandary (kwon´ dər ē) state of perplexity or uncertainty. *She was in a quandary over what to buy for her parents' anniversary.*

quatrain (kwo´ trān) stanza or poem of four lines. *He wrote a quatrain about baseball.*

quell (kwel) put down; overcome; subdue. *The police quelled the riot.*

quirk (kwerk) peculiar way of acting. *One of the sister's quirks is her garish taste in clothing.*

quorum (kwôr´ əm) minimum number of members of any society or assembly needed to transact business in a legal or binding way. *Since there was not a quorum at the meeting, we could not vote on the zoning issue.*

quoin (koin) outside angle or corner of a wall or building. *The builders bricked the quoins differently than the rest of the building.*

quittance (kwit´ 'ns) release from debt or obligation; the paper certifying this. *He received a quittance for the debt.*

quisling (kwiz´ ling) person who treacherously helps prepare the way for enemy occupation of his own country. *Quisling is another word for traitor.*

quirt (kwert) riding whip with a short, stout handle and a lash of braided leather. *The jockey used a quirt to make the horse run faster during the race.*

quiescent (kwē es´ ənt) inactive; quiet; still. *The little girl was very quiescent during the concert.*

queue (kū) a line, for example, of people or automobiles. *There was a long queue in front of the store for the grand opening.*

querulous (kwer´ ū ləs) complaining, fretful, peevish. *The elderly lady was very querulous when the clerk tried to help her.*

queasy (kwē´ zē) inclined to nausea; easily upset. *After I ate the pizza, my stomach felt queasy.*

Name: _____   Date: _____

Unit 17: "Q" Words: *Skills and Practice*

Directions: Write a **synonym** from the list of vocabulary words below on the line. A **synonym** is a word that means the same or nearly the same.

quaint	**quirt**	**quadruple**	**quoin**	**queue**
queasy	**quirk**	**quittance**	**qualm**	**quota**

1. line _____
3. portion _____
5. fourfold _____
7. whip _____
9. unusual _____

2. mannerism _____
4. cornerstone _____
6. receipt _____
8. doubt _____
10. squeamish _____

> **Did You Know?** *Questionnaire* has the base word *question*. *Question* came into the English language about 700 years ago from the French *questiun*. It can be traced back to the Latin word, *quaerere,* meaning "to seek, ask."

Directions: Write an **antonym** from the list of vocabulary words below on the line. An **antonym** is a word that means the opposite or nearly opposite.

quandary	**quell**	**query**	**quisling**	**querulous**
quiescent				

1. answer _____
3. certainty _____
5. boisterous _____

2. loyalist _____
4. encourage _____
6. easygoing _____

Directions: Write a sentence for each of the vocabulary words below on your own paper. Remember to check your spelling and punctuation.

questionnaire	**quadratic**	**quatrain**	**quorum**

Extend Your Vocabulary

1. Create a questionnaire about a subject that interests you. Survey 50 people, and make a graph of the results.
2. Write a narrative piece about someone who is facing a quandary.
3. Describe a quaint place you would like to visit. Use the Internet to help you.
4. List as many quislings in American history as you can. Why were they quislings?

67

Name: _____ Date: _____

Unit 17: "Q" Words: *Vocabulary Quiz*

Directions: Match each vocabulary word with the correct meaning. Write the word on the line next to the meaning.

quadruple	**questionnaire**	**quisling**	**qualm**	**quadratic**
quittance	**quandary**	**quaint**	**quell**	**quiescent**
quatrain	**quorum**	**quirk**	**query**	**querulous**
quoin	**quirt**	**queasy**	**quota**	**queue**

1. _____ release from debt or obligation; the paper certifying this

2. _____ written or printed list of questions used to gather information or to obtain a sampling of opinions

3. _____ peculiar way of acting

4. _____ share of the total due from or to a particular district, state, or person

5. _____ riding whip with a short, stout handle and a lash of braided leather

6. _____ strange or odd in an interesting, pleasing, or amusing way

7. _____ inclined to nausea; easily upset

8. _____ put down; overcome; subdue

9. _____ minimum number of members of any society or assembly needed to transact business in a legal or binding way

10. _____ consisting of four parts; including four parts or parties; four times

11. _____ outside angle or corner of a wall or building

12. _____ question; inquiry

13. _____ person who treacherously helps prepare the way for enemy occupation of his own country

14. _____ sudden disturbing feeling in the mind; uneasiness

15. _____ a line, for example, of people or automobiles

16. _____ state of perplexity or uncertainty

17. _____ inactive; quiet; still

18. _____ stanza or poem of four lines

19. _____ of or like a square

20. _____ complaining; fretful; peevish

Name: _____   Date: _____

Unit 18: "R" Words: *Vocabulary List and Alphabetizing*

reassure (rē´ ə shŏŏr´)   regrettable (ri gret´ ə bəl)

reliance (ri lī´ əns)   refinery (ri fīn´ ər ē)

recuperate (ri kōō´ pə rāt´)   receptacle (ri sep´ tə kəl)

reconcile (rek´ ən sīl´)   relinquish (ri ling´ kwish)

reminiscent (rem´ ə nis´ ənt)   respective (ri spek´ tiv)

reinstate (rē´ in stāt´)   repugnant (ri pug´ nənt)

retrograde (re´ trə grād´)   retrospect (re´ trə spekt´)

ricochet (rik´ ə shā´)   riddance (rid´ 'ns)

rigmarole (rig´ ə mə rōl´)   riven (riv´ ən)

rogue (rōg)   ruffian (ruf´ ē ən)

Directions: Write the above vocabulary words in alphabetical order below.

1. _____   11. _____

2. _____   12. _____

3. _____   13. _____

4. _____   14. _____

5. _____   15. _____

6. _____   16. _____

7. _____   17. _____

8. _____   18. _____

9. _____   19. _____

10. _____   20. _____

Unit 18: "R" Words: *Get the Facts!*

reassure (rē´ ə sho͝or´) restore to confidence. *The mother reassured the children after the thunderstorm.*

regrettable (ri gret´ ə bəl) deserving or giving cause for regret. *It was regrettable that you were involved in the car accident.*

reliance (ri lī´ əns) trust or dependence. *She has a reliance on her father when it comes to decision-making.*

refinery (ri fīn´ ər ē) building and machinery for purifying petroleum, sugar, or other things. *He worked at the local oil refinery.*

recuperate (ri ko͞o´ pə rāt´) recover from sickness, exhaustion, or loss. *It took her a few days to recuperate after the marathon race.*

receptacle (ri sep´ tə kəl) any container or place used to keep items contained conveniently. *They put the trash from their picnic into the receptacle.*

reconcile (rek´ ən sīl´) make friends again; settle a difference or quarrel. *The children reconciled after their fight.*

relinquish (ri ling´ kwish) give up; let go. *Reluctantly, the little girl relinquished the toy.*

reminiscent (rem´ ə nis´ ənt) recalling past persons or events. *The elderly men had a reminiscent talk about the good old days.*

respective (ri spek´ tiv) belong to each; particular. *The girls went to their respective bedrooms.*

reinstate (rē´ in stāt´) put back in a former position or condition; establish again. *He was reinstated into the organization as their president, five years after last holding the office.*

repugnant (ri pug´ nənt) disagreeable or offensive. *There was a repugnant smell coming from the trash can.*

retrograde (re´ trə grād´) moving backward; retreating. *The planet appeared to be moving in a retrograde fashion around the star.*

retrospect (re´ trə spekt´) survey of past time or events; thinking about the past. *In retrospect, she decided her father had been right.*

ricochet (rik´ ə shā´) move with a jumping or skipping motion. *The rocks ricocheted off the metal beam.*

riddance (rid´ 'ns) clearing away or out. *The riddance of the garbage dump was good for everyone.*

rigmarole (rig´ ə mə rōl´) foolish talk or activity; words or action without meaning. *Her essay answers were a bunch of rigmarole, making it obvious that she hadn't studied the material.*

riven (riv´ ən) torn apart; split. *The riven school banner was a sad sight.*

rogue (rōg) dishonest or unprincipled person; mischievous person. *He was a rogue when it came to business; no one could trust him.*

ruffian (ruf´ ē ən) brutal, rough, or cruel person; hoodlum. *The homeless youth was the ruffian of the neighborhood.*

Name: _____ Date: _____

Unit 18: "R" Words: *Skills and Practice*

Directions: Write a **synonym** from the list of vocabulary words below on the line. A **synonym** is a word that means the same or nearly the same.

regrettable	**reconcile**	**ruffian**	**riddance**	**respective**
rigmarole	**reassure**	**rogue**	**ricochet**	**receptacle**
reminiscent	**repugnant**			

1. sorrowful _____
2. reunite _____
3. removal _____
4. guarantee _____
5. container _____
6. distasteful _____
7. recall _____
8. individual _____
9. rebound _____
10. nonsense _____
11. rascal _____
12. bully _____

Did You Know? The prefix *re-* can mean "back" in such words as *recall, reflect,* or *repay.* It can also mean "again" in such words as *reappear, recopy,* or *redo.*

Directions: Write an **antonym** from the list of vocabulary words below on the line. An **antonym** is a word that means the opposite or nearly opposite.

riven	**retrograde**	**recuperate**	**relinquish**	**reliance**

1. resist _____
2. repaired _____
3. mistrust _____
4. onward _____
5. regress _____

Directions: Write a sentence for each of the vocabulary words below on your own paper. Remember to check your spelling and punctuation.

refinery   **reinstate**   **retrospect**

Extend Your Vocabulary

1. If there were a ruffian in your class, what could you do? Why? Write about it.
2. List some repugnant smells or odors. Why are some odors repugnant to you and others aren't?
3. Research and write about oil refineries. Include their locations, values, problems, and impact on the environment.
4. Describe a situation that was regrettable to you. What could you have done differently?

Name: _____ Date: _____

Unit 18: "R" Words: *Vocabulary Quiz*

Directions: Match each vocabulary word with the correct meaning. Write the word on the line next to the meaning.

reassure	**regrettable**	**reliance**	**recuperate**	**ruffian**
receptacle	**reconcile**	**relinquish**	**reminiscent**	**riven**
respective	**reinstate**	**repugnant**	**retrograde**	**rogue**
retrospect	**ricochet**	**riddance**	**rigmarole**	**refinery**

1. _____ disagreeable or offensive

2. _____ restore to confidence

3. _____ put back in a former position or condition; establish again

4. _____ building and machinery for purifying petroleum, sugar, or other things

5. _____ clearing away or out

6. _____ make friends again; settle a difference or quarrel

7. _____ moving backward; retreating

8. _____ deserving or giving cause for regret

9. _____ foolish talk or activity; words or action without meaning

10. _____ give up; let go

11. _____ dishonest or unprincipled person; mischievous person

12. _____ belong to each; particular

13. _____ survey of past time or events; thinking about the past

14. _____ recover from sickness, exhaustion, or loss

15. _____ torn apart, split

16. _____ any container or place used to keep items contained conveniently

17. _____ brutal, rough, or cruel person; hoodlum

18. _____ recalling past persons or events

19. _____ move with a jumping or skipping motion

20. _____ trust or dependence

Name: _____   Date: _____

Unit 19: "S" Words: *Vocabulary List and Alphabetizing*

secrecy (sē´ krə sē)

subtle (sut´ 'l)

sire (sīr)

submerge (səb mûrj´)

studious (stoō´ dē əs)

scrimmage (skrim´ ij)

sieve (siv)

soluble (sol´ yə bəl)

stupefy (stoō´ pə fī´)

substantial (səb stan´ shəl)

sentimental (sen´ tə ment´ 'l)

scoundrel (skoun´ drəl)

strenuous (stren´ ū əs)

sullen (sul´ ən)

supplement (sup´ lə mənt)

subsidy (sub´ sə dē)

sinister (sin´ is tər)

strewn (stroōn)

superlative (sə pûr´ lə tiv)

subsequent (sub´ si kwənt´)

Directions: Write the above vocabulary words in alphabetical order below.

1. _____
2. _____
3. _____
4. _____
5. _____
6. _____
7. _____
8. _____
9. _____
10. _____

11. _____
12. _____
13. _____
14. _____
15. _____
16. _____
17. _____
18. _____
19. _____
20. _____

Unit 19: "S" Words: *Get the Facts!*

secrecy (sē´ krə sē) condition of being secret or of being kept secret. *He maintained secrecy regarding his company's marketing strategy.*

sentimental (sen´ tə ment´ 'l) having or showing much tender feeling. *Christmas is a sentimental time for me.*

subtle (sut´ 'l) not obvious; delicate; fine. *In da Vinci's painting, "Mona Lisa" has a subtle smile.*

scoundrel (skoun´ drəl) wicked person without honor or good principles. *The villains in a story are usually scoundrels.*

sire (sīr) male ancestor, male parent. *Adam was the sire of Cain and Abel in the Bible.*

strenuous (stren´ ū əs) very active; requiring much energy. *Getting in shape for the Olympics is strenuous.*

submerge (səb mûrj´) put under water; cover with water. *No one could see the submarine because it was submerged in the ocean.*

sullen (sul´ ən) silent because of bad humor or anger. *The sullen child pouted in his chair.*

studious (stoo´ dē əs) fond of study; showing careful consideration; careful. *Tyler is very studious when it comes to science.*

supplement (sup´ lə mənt) something added to complete something or to make it larger or better. *The Sunday newspaper has many supplements, especially during the holidays.*

scrimmage (skrim´ ij) rough fight or struggle. *There was a scrimmage between the British and the colonists.*

subsidy (sub´ sə dē) grant or contribution of money, especially one made by a government. *The school received a subsidy for their science program.*

sieve (siv) utensil with many tiny holes for separating the finer from the coarser parts of a substance. *My mother uses her sieve to drain pasta.*

sinister (sin´ is tər) threatening; bad; evil; dishonest. *The villain in the movie had a sinister look on his face.*

soluble (sol´ yə bəl) capable of being dissolved. *Sugar is soluble in water.*

strewn (stroon) scattered or sprinkled. *The ground was strewn with litter.*

stupefy (stoo´ pə fī´) make stupid, dull; astound; overwhelm with shock. *The people were stupefied with the news about the death of the president.*

superlative (sə pûr´ lə tiv) of the highest kind; above all others. *Her superlative sewing skills were evident in the beautiful quilt she entered at the fair.*

substantial (səb stan´ shəl) material; real; large; important. *He lost a substantial amount of money in the bet.*

subsequent (sub´ si kwənt´) after; following; later. *The test given subsequent to the lesson showed that the students had paid attention in class.*

Name: _____   Date: _____

Unit 19: "S" Words: *Skills and Practice*

Directions: Write a **synonym** from the list of vocabulary words below on the line. A **synonym** is a word that means the same or nearly the same.

sieve	scoundrel	strewn	scrimmage	supplement
sire	stupefy	studious	subsidy	superlative

1. supreme _____   2. forefather _____
3. thoughtful _____   4. rogue _____
5. grant _____   6. senseless _____
7. addition _____   8. struggle _____
9. strainer _____   10. scattered _____

> **Did You Know?** The prefix *sub-* means "under or below." Many of our words, such as *subnormal,* begin with this prefix. It can also mean "lower or subordinate," as in *subcommittee.*

Directions: Write an **antonym** from the list of vocabulary words below on the line. An **antonym** is a word that means the opposite or nearly opposite.

submerge	sentimental	subtle	substantial	sullen
strenuous	subsequent	sinister		

1. surface _____   2. pleasant _____
3. practical _____   4. virtuous _____
5. overt _____   6. preceding _____
7. unimportant _____   8. easy _____

Directions: Write a sentence for each of the vocabulary words below on your own paper. Remember to check your spelling and punctuation.

secrecy   soluble

Extend Your Vocabulary

1. Experiment with items that are soluble in water. Write about your discoveries.
2. List the skills that a studious student needs to be successful.
3. Write about a time when you were sentimental. Include when it happened, where you were, and what happened to cause you to feel that way.
4. Make a list of different words for scoundrel. Tell about a scoundrel in a book you have read. What made him a scoundrel? Was he successful, or did the "good guys" win?

75

Name: _____ Date: _____

Unit 19: "S" Words: *Vocabulary Quiz*

Directions: Match each vocabulary word with the correct meaning. Write the word on the line next to the meaning.

secrecy	**sentimental**	**subtle**	**scoundrel**	**stupefy**
strenuous	**submerge**	**sullen**	**studious**	**sieve**
supplement	**scrimmage**	**subsidy**	**sinister**	**strewn**
superlative	**subsequent**	**soluble**	**substantial**	**sire**

1. _____ utensil with many tiny holes for separating the finer from the coarser parts of a substance.

2. _____ condition of being secret or of being kept secret

3. _____ scattered or sprinkled

4. _____ very active; requiring much energy

5. _____ grant or contribution of money, especially one made by a government

6. _____ not obvious; delicate; fine

7. _____ make stupid, dull; astound; overwhelm with shock

8. _____ fond of study; showing careful consideration; careful

9. _____ threatening; bad; evil; dishonest

10. _____ wicked person without honor or good principles

11. _____ of the highest kind; above all others

12. _____ something added to complete something or to make it larger or better

13. _____ after; following; later

14. _____ rough fight or struggle

15. _____ capable of being dissolved

16. _____ male ancestor; male parent

17. _____ silent because of bad humor or anger

18. _____ having or showing much tender feeling

19. _____ material; real; large; important

20. _____ put under water; cover with water

76

Name: _____   Date: _____

Unit 20: "T" Words: *Vocabulary List and Alphabetizing*

toil (toil)	torrent (tôr´ ənt)
transmit (trans mit´)	transfusion (trans fū´ zhən)
turmoil (tər´ moil´)	tangible (tan´ jə bəl)
tether (te*th*´ ər)	transpose (trans pōz´)
trestle (tres´ əl)	tumult (too´ mult)
tithe (tī*th*)	transcend (tran send´)
taut (tôt)	tabor (tā´ bər)
tandem (tan´ dəm)	tankard (tang´ kərd)
tantalize (tan´ tə līz´)	transparent (trans per´ ənt)
tempest (tem´ pist)	tenacious (tə nā´ shəs)

Directions: Write the above vocabulary words in alphabetical order below.

1. _____   11. _____

2. _____   12. _____

3. _____   13. _____

4. _____   14. _____

5. _____   15. _____

6. _____   16. _____

7. _____   17. _____

8. _____   18. _____

9. _____   19. _____

10. _____   20. _____

77

Unit 20: "T" Words: *Get the Facts!*

toil (toil) work hard; move with weariness, pain, or difficulty. *The miners toiled in the mines many hours each day.*

torrent (tôr´ ənt) violent, rushing stream; heavy downpour. *A torrent of lava rushed from the volcano.*

transmit (trans mit´) send over; pass on; pass along. *Radio waves are transmitted through the air.*

transfusion (trans fū´ zhən) transfer of blood from one person or animal to another. *During the operation, the lady needed a transfusion.*

turmoil (tər´ moil´) state of agitation or commotion; tumult; disturbance. *The boy was filled with turmoil and had to be removed from the room.*

tangible (tan´ jə bəl) real; actual; definite. *Candy is a tangible reward.*

tether (te*th*´ ər) rope or chain for fastening an animal so that it can graze or move only within a certain limit. *The tether on the horse broke, allowing him to gallop away.*

transpose (trans pōz´) change the position or order of. *The little child transposed the letters in his name.*

trestle (tres´ əl) framework similar to a saw-horse, used as support for a table top platform. *The trestle needs to be strong for the marble table top.*

tumult (tōō´ mult) noise or uproar. *The tumult of the party caused the neighbors to call the police.*

tithe (tī*th*) make or pledge a payment for the support of the church. *She tithed one-tenth of her yearly income to the church.*

transcend (tran send´) go beyond the limits or powers of; be above; surpass. *The majesty of the pyramids transcends words.*

taut (tôt) tightly drawn; tense. *When he slid down the taut rope, it caused a rope burn on his hands.*

tabor (tā´ bər) small drum, used especially with a pipe or fife played as an accompaniment. *There is a picture about the American Revolution showing three soldiers, one of whom is playing a tabor.*

tandem (tan´ dəm) having two seats or parts, for example, arranged one behind the other. *The couple enjoyed riding a tandem bicycle.*

tankard (tang´ kərd) large drinking mug with a handle and a hinged cover. *The king was drinking mead from a tankard.*

tantalize (tan´ tə līz´) torment by keeping something desired in sight but out of reach or by holding out hopes that are repeatedly disappointed. *He tantalized the hungry man by eating in front of him.*

transparent (trans per´ ənt) letting light through so that things on the other side can be distinctly seen. *Window glass is transparent.*

tempest (tem´ pist) a violent windstorm, usually accompanied by rain, hail, or snow. *The tempest caused great damage to the town.*

tenacious (tə nā´ shəs) holding fast; stubborn; persistent. *She is a tenacious salesperson, which makes her a successful realtor.*

Name: _____ Date: _____

Unit 20: "T" Words: *Skills and Practice*

Directions: Write a **synonym** from the list of vocabulary words below on the line. A **synonym** is a word that means the same or nearly the same.

torrent	tantalize	tankard	transcend	toil
transpose	tempest	tumult	tabor	

1. exceed _____
2. mug _____
3. flood _____
4. drum _____
5. labor _____
6. tease _____
7. interchange _____
8. commotion _____
9. windstorm _____

Did You Know? *Tantalize* came from the name of Tantalus, a king in a Greek myth. After his death, his spirit was punished by having to stand in water under branches of a tree filled with fruit. When Tantalus reached for some fruit, it receded from his grasp. When he bent down to drink, the water drained away.

Directions: Write an **antonym** from the list of vocabulary words below on the line. An **antonym** is a word that means the opposite or nearly opposite.

turmoil	transmit	transparent	taut	tangible	tenacious

1. opaque _____
2. calmness _____
3. loose _____
4. retain _____
5. abstract _____
6. yielding _____

Directions: Write a sentence for each of the vocabulary words below on your own paper. Remember to check your spelling and punctuation.

transfusion	tether	tandem	trestle	tithe

Extend Your Vocabulary

1. Explain the meaning of the phrase "at the end of one's tether."
2. Research and write about the picture showing three soldiers marching during the American Revolution. One is carrying a flag, another a tabor, and the last a fife.
3. Write about the pros and cons of blood transfusions. Use a T-chart or Venn diagram to help organize your thoughts.
4. Write a narrative piece about a time you toiled for something. Include how you felt, what happened, and so on.

Name: _____ Date: _____

Unit 20: "T" Words: *Vocabulary Quiz*

Directions: Match each vocabulary word with the correct meaning. Write the word on the line next to the meaning.

torrent	transmit	transfusion	turmoil	toil
tangible	tether	transcend	transparent	tabor
tandem	tankard	tantalize	transpose	tithe
trestle	tumult	tempest	tenacious	taut

1. _____ having two seats, parts, animals, etc., arranged one behind the other

2. _____ violent, rushing stream; heavy downpour

3. _____ change the position or order of

4. _____ state of agitation or commotion; tumult; disturbance

5. _____ noise or uproar

6. _____ go beyond the limits or powers of; be above; surpass

7. _____ violent windstorm, usually accompanied by rain, hail, or snow

8. _____ small drum, used especially with a pipe or fife played as an accompaniment

9. _____ large drinking mug with a handle and a hinged cover

10. _____ work hard; move with weariness, pain, or difficulty

11. _____ torment by keeping something desired in sight but out of reach or by holding out hopes that are repeatedly disappointed

12. _____ send over; pass on; pass along

13. _____ make or pledge a payment for the support of the church

14. _____ letting light through so that things on the other side can be distinctly seen

15. _____ holding fast; stubborn; persistent

16. _____ real; actual; definite

17. _____ tightly drawn; tense

18. _____ transfer of blood from one person or animal to another

19. _____ framework similar to a sawhorse, used as support for a table top platform

20. _____ rope or chain for fastening an animal so it can graze or move only within a certain limit

Name: _____ Date: _____

Unit 21: "U" Words: *Vocabulary List and Alphabetizing*

unravel (un rav´ əl)

unanimous (yōō nan´ ə məs)

uncouth (un kōōth´)

ultimatum (ul´ tə māt´ əm)

unbiased (un bī´ əst)

undaunted (un dôn´ tid)

undergo (un´ dər gō´)

unfurl (un fûrl´)

urbane (ûr bān´)

unrest (un rest´)

utmost (ut´ mōst)

undertone (un´ dər tōn´)

undertake (un´ dər tāk´)

upheaval (up hē´ vəl)

uncanny (un kan´ ē)

undeniable (un´ di nī´ ə bəl)

undermine (un´ dər mīn´)

unequivocal (un´ ē kwiv´ ə kəl)

unison (ū´ nə sən)

unintentional (un in ten´ shə nəl)

Directions: Write the above vocabulary words in alphabetical order below.

1. _____

2. _____

3. _____

4. _____

5. _____

6. _____

7. _____

8. _____

9. _____

10. _____

11. _____

12. _____

13. _____

14. _____

15. _____

16. _____

17. _____

18. _____

19. _____

20. _____

Unit 21 "U" Words: *Get the Facts!*

unravel (un ravˊ əl) separate the threads of; pull apart; come apart. *Her braid is unraveling because the ribbon fell off.*

utmost (utˊ mōst) greatest possible; greatest; highest. *Exercise is of the utmost importance to a healthy life.*

unanimous (yo͞o nanˊ ə məs) in complete accord or agreement; agreed. *The children were unanimous in their decision about the best field trip.*

undertone (unˊ dər tōnˊ) low or very quiet tone. *They talked in undertones during the movie.*

uncouth (un ko͞othˊ) not refined; awkward; clumsy; crude. *The man was not a popular dinner guest because of his uncouth manners.*

undertake (unˊ dər tākˊ) set about; try; attempt. *He will undertake a new job next month.*

ultimatum (ulˊ tə mātˊ əm) a final offer or demand given with the threat of severe penalties if refused. *She was given an ultimatum to pay the fine or go to jail.*

upheaval (up hēˊ vəl) a sudden or violent agitation; great turmoil. *The flood caused a great upheaval for many months.*

unbiased (un bīˊ əst) impartial; fair. *A teacher needs to be unbiased in the classroom.*

uncanny (un kanˊ ē) strange and mysterious. *He has an uncanny way of always being at the wrong place at the wrong time.*

undaunted (un dônˊ tid) not afraid; not discouraged; fearless. *The toddler was undaunted by the large dog.*

undeniable (unˊ di nīˊ ə bəl) beyond denial or dispute. *The attorney's belief in his client's innocence was undeniable.*

undergo (unˊ dər gōˊ) endure. *The older gentleman will undergo the operation next week.*

undermine (unˊ dər mīnˊ) weaken by secret or unfair means. *Gossip undermined her reputation.*

unfurl (un fûrlˊ) spread out; shake out. *Unfurl the blanket for the picnic.*

unequivocal (unˊ ē kwivˊ ə kəl) clear; plain. *He gave an unequivocal answer of "not guilty."*

urbane (ûr bānˊ) courteous; refined. *Her grandmother always shows urbane manners.*

unison (ūˊ nə sən) agreement; at the same time. *The choir sang in unison.*

unrest (un restˊ) lack of ease and quiet; restlessness. *There was much unrest just before the rebellion.*

unintentional (un in tenˊ shə nəl) not intentional; not done purposely. *The breaking of the dish was unintentional.*

Name: _____ Date: _____

Unit 21 "U" Words: *Skills and Practice*

Directions: Write a **synonym** from the list of vocabulary words below on the line. A **synonym** is a word that means the same or nearly the same.

unison	**unequivocal**	**upheaval**	**undergo**	**urbane**
unravel	**undeniable**	**uncanny**	**unfurl**	

1. turmoil _____
2. weird _____
3. suffer _____
4. agreement _____
5. certain _____
6. separate _____
7. unfold _____
8. plain _____
9. elegant _____

> **Did You Know?** The prefix *un-* means "not," and the prefix *under-* means "below."

Directions: Write an **antonym** from the list of vocabulary words below on the line. An **antonym** is a word that means the opposite or nearly opposite.

undertake	**utmost**	**undaunted**	**unrest**	**uncouth**
unanimous	**unbiased**	**unintentional**		

1. disagreed _____
2. avoid _____
3. prejudiced _____
4. littlest _____
5. refined _____
6. fearful _____
7. planned _____
8. ease _____

Directions: Write a sentence for each of the vocabulary words below on your own paper. Remember to check your spelling and punctuation.

undertone	**ultimatum**	**undermine**

Extend Your Vocabulary

1. Make as many opposites as you can using the prefix *un-*. For example: biased/unbiased, bearable/unbearable.
2. List some hardships the pioneers had to undergo in America.
3. There have been times of unrest in America's history. Write about one of those times.
4. Write a persuasive piece about whether someone can be unbiased in politics.

Name: _____ Date: _____

Unit 21: "U" Words: *Vocabulary Quiz*

Directions: Match each vocabulary word with the correct meaning. Write the word on the line next to the meaning.

unravel	utmost	unanimous	undertone	uncouth
undertake	ultimatum	upheaval	unbiased	uncanny
unison	undeniable	undergo	undermine	unfurl
unrest	unequivocal	unintentional	undaunted	urbane

1. _____ not afraid; not discouraged; fearless

2. _____ in complete accord or agreement; agreed

3. _____ weaken by secret or unfair means

4. _____ set about; try; attempt

5. _____ agreement; at the same time

6. _____ sudden or violent agitation; great turmoil

7. _____ endure

8. _____ separate the threads of; pull apart; come apart

9. _____ courteous; refined

10. _____ impartial; fair

11. _____ clear; plain

12. _____ low or very quiet tone

13. _____ beyond denial or dispute

14. _____ greatest possible; greatest; highest

15. _____ not intentional; not done purposely

16. _____ final offer or demand given with the threat of severe penalties if refused

17. _____ spread out; shake out

18. _____ not refined; awkward; clumsy; crude

19. _____ strange and mysterious

20. _____ lack of ease and quiet; restlessness

Name: _____   Date: _____

Unit 22: "V" Words: *Vocabulary List and Alphabetizing*

vicinity (və sin´ ə tē)	vagabond (vag´ ə bond´)
vigorous (vig´ ər əs)	vengeance (ven´ jəns)
vestibule (ves´ tə byo͞ol´)	valiant (val´ yənt)
veranda (və ran´ də)	vitality (vī tal´ ə tē)
valise (və lēs´)	veneer (və nir´)
versatile (vûr´ sə təl)	vulnerable (vul´ nər ə bəl)
vacillate (vas´ ə lāt)	vacuity (va kyo͞o´ ə tē)
volition (vō lish´ ən)	valance (val´ əns)
valedictory (val´ ə dik´ tər ē)	valet (va lā´)
vanquish (vang´ kwish)	vertigo (vûr´ ti gō´)

Directions: Write the above vocabulary words in alphabetical order below.

1. _____	11. _____
2. _____	12. _____
3. _____	13. _____
4. _____	14. _____
5. _____	15. _____
6. _____	16. _____
7. _____	17. _____
8. _____	18. _____
9. _____	19. _____
10. _____	20. _____

85

Unit 22: "V" Words: *Get the Facts!*

vicinity (və sin´ ə tē) region near or about a place. *She lives in the vicinity of Madison School.*

vagabond (vag´ ə bond´) idle wanderer; wanderer. *The vagabond traveled by jumping on freight trains.*

vigorous (vig´ ər əs) full of vigor; strong and active; energetic; forceful. *He was a vigorous speaker at the conference.*

vengeance (ven´ jəns) punishment in return for a wrong; revenge. *He promised vengeance against the man who had wronged him.*

vestibule (ves´ tə byool´) passage or hall between the outer door and the inside of a building. *He waited in the vestibule of the auditorium for his date.*

valiant (val´ yənt) brave; courageous. *The soldier was valiant in his efforts during the war.*

veranda (və ran´ də) large porch along one or more sides of a house. *We sat and drank iced tea on the veranda.*

vitality (vī tal´ ə tē) vital force; power to live. *Her vitality is strong even after the operation.*

valise (və lēs´) traveling bag to hold clothes or other personal belongings. *The salesman carried his valise onto the train.*

veneer (və nir´) cover with a thin layer of fine wood or other material. *The table is veneered with cherry wood.*

versatile (vûr´ sə təl) able to do many things well. *He is very versatile when it comes to working with his hands.*

vulnerable (vul´ nər ə bəl) sensitive to criticism, temptations, or influences. *She is vulnerable about her weight problem.*

vacillate (vas´ ə lāt) waver in mind or opinion. *I was vacillating about my decision regarding the purchase of a new car.*

vacuity (va kyoo´ ə tē) emptiness; an empty space. *The vacuity of an abandoned house makes it an easy target for vandalism.*

volition (vō lish´ ən) act of willing; decision. *She did the job of her own volition.*

valance (val´ əns) short drapery over the top of a window. *Her mother made her a ruffled valance for her bedroom window.*

valedictory (val´ ə dik´ tər ē) farewell address, especially at the graduation exercises of a school or college. *He gave the valedictory at his college graduation.*

valet (va lā´) servant who takes care of a man's clothes and gives him personal service. *The well-groomed king has several valets to attend him.*

vanquish (vang´ kwish) conquer; defeat; overcome. *The boy tried to vanquish his fear of heights by climbing the tall tree.*

vertigo (vûr´ ti gō´) dizziness; giddiness. *She doesn't care to climb ladders because she suffers from vertigo.*

Name: _____ Date: _____

Unit 22: "V" Words: *Skills and Practice*

Directions: Write a **synonym** from the list of vocabulary words below on the line. A **synonym** is a word that means the same or nearly the same.

valet	**volition**	**vagabond**	**vengeance**	**vacuity**
valance	**vertigo**	**valedictory**	**veranda**	**vestibule**

1. vacuum _____
2. servant _____
3. curtain _____
4. decision _____
5. farewell _____
6. tramp _____
7. dizziness _____
8. revenge _____
9. porch _____
10. hall _____

> **Did You Know?** The root *vag*, which means "wander," came from Latin. Some of our English words that came from the Latin root are *vagabond, vagrant,* and *vagary.*

Directions: Write an **antonym** from the list of vocabulary words below on the line. An **antonym** is a word that means the opposite or nearly opposite.

vanquish	**vacillate**	**valiant**	**versatile**	**vulnerable**
vigorous				

1. steadfast _____
2. afraid _____
3. surrender _____
4. limited _____
5. weak _____
6. secure _____

Directions: Write a sentence for each of the vocabulary words below on your own paper. Remember to check your spelling and punctuation.

vicinity	**valise**	**veneer**	**vitality**

Extend Your Vocabulary

1. Draw a map of the vicinity of your home. Label streets, places of business, stores, and so on.
2. List some occupations that would require you to be vigorous.
3. Write a narrative piece about a time when you were valiant.
4. Discuss why there were so many verandas in the South. Write about it.

Name: _____   Date: _____

Unit 22: "V" Words: *Vocabulary Quiz*

Directions: Match each vocabulary word with the correct meaning. Write the word on the line next to the meaning.

vicinity	**vagabond**	**vigorous**	**vengeance**	**vestibule**
valiant	**veranda**	**vitality**	**valise**	**veneer**
versatile	**vulnerable**	**vacillate**	**vacuity**	**volition**
valance	**valedictory**	**valet**	**vanquish**	**vertigo**

1. _____ sensitive to criticism, temptations, or influences

2. _____ region near or about a place

3. _____ act of willing; decision

4. _____ punishment in return for a wrong; revenge

5. _____ waver in mind or opinion

6. _____ idle wanderer; wanderer

7. _____ servant who takes care of a man's clothes and gives him personal service

8. _____ traveling bag to hold clothes and other personal belongings

9. _____ short drapery over the top of a window

10. _____ large porch along one or more sides of a house

11. _____ conquer; defeat; overcome

12. _____ able to do many things well

13. _____ emptiness; an empty space

14. _____ full of vigor; strong and active; energetic; forceful

15. _____ farewell address, especially at the graduation exercise of a school or college

16. _____ brave; courageous

17. _____ dizziness; giddiness

18. _____ cover with a thin layer of fine wood or other material

19. _____ passage or hall between the outer door and the inside of a building

20. _____ vital force; power to live

Name: _____   Date: _____

Unit 23: "W" Words: *Vocabulary List and Alphabetizing*

warden (wôrd´ 'n)   wean (wēn)

waif (wāf)   writhe (rīth)

waft (woft)   wallop (wo´ ləp)

wanton (wont´ 'n)   warble (wôr´ bəl)

wayfarer (wā´ fer´ ər)   welter (wel´ tər)

wheedle (hwēd´ 'l)   wieldy (wēl´ dē)

winsome (win´ səm)   woeful (wō´ fəl)

wraith (rāth)   wrath (rath)

withstand (with stand´)   wince (wins)

whorl (hwôrl)   warrior (wôr´ ē ər)

Directions: Write the above vocabulary words in alphabetical order below.

1. _____   11. _____

2. _____   12. _____

3. _____   13. _____

4. _____   14. _____

5. _____   15. _____

6. _____   16. _____

7. _____   17. _____

8. _____   18. _____

9. _____   19. _____

10. _____   20. _____

Unit 23: "W" Words: *Get the Facts!*

warden (wôrd´ 'n) the official in charge of a prison. *The new warden is to start his prison duties next month.*

wean (wēn) accustom a person to do without something; cause to turn away. *She weaned herself from smoking cigarettes.*

waif (wāf) homeless or neglected child. *Did you see that waif in the deserted park?*

writhe (rīth) twist and turn; twist about. *The worm writhed around my finger.*

waft (woft) carry over water or through air. *The enticing aromas from the kitchen wafted through the house.*

wallop (wo´ ləp) hit very hard; strike with a vigorous blow. *He walloped the ball over the fence.*

wanton (wont´ 'n) done in a reckless, heartless, or malicious way. *It was a wanton waste of food to throw away nearly half a pizza.*

warble (wôr´ bəl) sing with trills, quavers, or melodious tunes. *The songbird warbled in the tree.*

wayfarer (wā´ fer´ ər) traveler. *The wayfarer traveled through the Orient.*

welter (wel´ tər) to roll or tumble about; a commotion; turmoil. *There was a welter of people at the rock concert.*

wheedle (hwēd´ 'l) persuade by flattery, smooth words, or caresses; coax. *The boys wheedled their parents into letting them go to the movies on a school night.*

wieldy (wēl´ dē) easily controlled or handled; manageable. *The wieldy package was easy to carry.*

winsome (win´ səm) charming; attractive; pleasing. *She has a winsome smile.*

woeful (wō´ fəl) full of woe; sad; sorrowful; wretched. *The lady had a woeful expression on her face after the death of her dog.*

wraith (rāth) specter; ghost. *I thought I saw a wraith in the cemetery.*

wrath (rath) very great anger; rage. *The man was full of wrath at the injustice of the crime.*

withstand (with stand´) stand against; resist; oppose; endure. *Bears withstand winter weather by hibernating.*

wince (wins) draw back suddenly; flinch slightly. *The child winced when she received a shot.*

whorl (hwôrl) anything that circles or turns on or around something else. *All fingerprints have different patterns of whorls, which makes each one unique.*

warrior (wôr´ ē ər) soldier. *The warriors fought a brave battle.*

Name: _____ Date: _____

Unit 23: "W" Words: *Skills and Practice*

Directions: Write a **synonym** from the list of vocabulary words below on the line. A **synonym** is a word that means the same or nearly the same.

warble	**warden**	**wayfarer**	**wanton**	**wraith**
wallop	**waft**	**writhe**	**waif**	**welter**

1. strike _____   2. chirp _____
3. sail _____   4. jailer _____
5. squirm _____   6. traveler _____
7. ragamuffin _____   8. malicious _____
9. confusion _____   10. spook _____

> **Did You Know?** *Winsome* comes from the Old English *wynsum,* which comes from *wynn* meaning "joy."

Directions: Write an **antonym** from the list of vocabulary words below on the line. An **antonym** is a word that means the opposite or nearly opposite.

woeful	**winsome**	**wrath**	**warrior**	**withstand**
wieldy	**wheedle**			

1. coerce _____   2. pacifist _____
3. wild _____   4. patience _____
5. repulsive _____   6. delightful _____
7. succumb _____

Directions: Write a sentence for each of the vocabulary words below on your own paper. Remember to check your spelling and punctuation.

wean	**wince**	**whorl**

Extend Your Vocabulary

1. Why can humans withstand so many hardships, such as tornadoes, hurricanes, and floods? Write your reasons.
2. List as many words as you can for sad, such as *woeful.*
3. Research fingerprints. Why are all whorls different? Can you change them? Write a mini-report.
4. Find a picture of a bird that warbles.

Name: _____ Date: _____

Unit 23: "W" Words: *Vocabulary Quiz*

Directions: Match each vocabulary word with the correct meaning. Write the word on the line next to the meaning.

warden	**withstand**	**wean**	**woeful**	**writhe**
wallop	**wanton**	**waft**	**wrath**	**wieldy**
warble	**wayfarer**	**waif**	**welter**	**wraith**
wheedle	**winsome**	**wince**	**whorl**	**warrior**

1. _____ charming; attractive; pleasing

2. _____ official in charge of a prison

3. _____ easily controlled or handled; manageable

4. _____ twist and turn; twist about

5. _____ very great anger; rage

6. _____ hit very hard; strike with a vigorous blow

7. _____ stand against; resist; oppose; endure

8. _____ sing with trills, quavers, or melodious tunes

9. _____ anything that circles or turns on or around something else

10. _____ persuade by flattery, smooth words, or caresses; coax

11. _____ specter; ghost

12. _____ accustom a person to do without something; cause to turn away

13. _____ full of woe; sad; sorrowful; wretched

14. _____ homeless or neglected child

15. _____ draw back suddenly; flinch slightly

16. _____ carry over water or through the air

17. _____ soldier

18. _____ done in a reckless, heartless, or malicious way

19. _____ to roll or tumble about; a commotion; turmoil

20. _____ traveler

Name: _____ Date: _____

Unit 24: "X" (Ex) Words: *Vocabulary List and Alphabetizing*

existence (eg zis′ təns)

exquisite (eks′ kwiz it)

expenditure (ek spen′ di chər)

extremity (ek strem′ ə tē)

exultation (egz′ əl tā′ shən)

extraneous (ek strā′ nē əs)

exalt (eg zôlt′)

exhort (eg zôrt′)

exonerate (eg zon′ ər āt′)

expound (ek spound′)

exert (eg zûrt′)

extract (ek strakt′)

exasperate (eg zas′ pər āt′)

exuberant (eg zōō′ bər ənt)

explicit (eks plis′ it)

extortion (ek stôr′ shən)

excise (ek sīz′)

excruciating (eks krōō′ shē′ āt′ ing)

exorbitant (eg zôr′ bi tənt)

extemporaneous (eks′ tem′ pə rā′ nē əs)

Directions: Write the above vocabulary words in alphabetical order below.

1. _____

2. _____

3. _____

4. _____

5. _____

6. _____

7. _____

8. _____

9. _____

10. _____

11. _____

12. _____

13. _____

14. _____

15. _____

16. _____

17. _____

18. _____

19. _____

20. _____

Unit 24: "X" (Ex) Words: *Get the Facts!*

existence (eg zis´ təns) being; a being real. *Do you believe in the existence of angels?*

exert (eg zûrt´) put into use; use fully. *A football player exerts much strength.*

exquisite (eks´ kwiz it) very lovely; delicate; most admirable. *The roses in her bridal bouquet are exquisite.*

extract (ek strakt´) pull out or draw out, usually with some effort. *The detective extracted a confession from the criminal.*

expenditure (ek spen´ di chər) a using up; a spending. *Her expenditure for decorations was $50.00.*

exasperate (eg zas´ pər āt´) irritate very much; annoy greatly; make angry. *His continued whining exasperated his mom.*

extremity (ek strem´ ə tē) the very end; farthest possible place; last point or part. *The North Pole is the last extremity of the Northern Hemisphere.*

exuberant (eg zoo´ bər ənt) abounding in health and high spirits; overflowing with good cheer. *He is in an exuberant mood today.*

exultation (egz´ əl tā´ shən) an exulting; great rejoicing. *There was great exultation over the state championships.*

explicit (eks plis´ it) clearly expressed; definite. *He gave explicit directions on how to make a birdhouse.*

extraneous (ek strā´ nē əs) not essential. *John's extra credit presentation is extraneous since he already has an "A" for the class.*

extortion (ek stôr´ shən) obtaining by threats, force, fraud, or wrong use of authority. *The man used extortion to obtain money from the local store owners.*

exalt (eg zôlt´) make high in rank, honor, power, character, or quality; praise; glorify. *The queen was exalted by her countrymen.*

excise (ek sīz´) cut out. *The dentist excised the girl's wisdom teeth.*

excruciating (eks kroo´ shē´ āt´ ing) causing great suffering. *The recovery of the man after the near-fatal accident was excruciating.*

exhort (eg zôrt´) urge strongly; advise or warn earnestly. *The doctor exhorted the patient on the value of healthy eating.*

exonerate (eg zon´ ər āt´) free from blame. *The defendant was exonerated in court.*

exorbitant (eg zôr´ bi tənt) much too high; unreasonably excessive. *That was an exorbitant price to pay for a pair of shoes.*

expound (ek spound´) make clear; explain. *The teacher expounded on the steps for long division.*

extemporaneous (eks´ tem´ pə rā´ nē əs) spoken or done without preparation. *She gave an extemporaneous speech to the audience when she received the award.*

94

Name: _____   Date: _____

Unit 24: "X" (Ex) Words: *Skills and Practice*

Directions: Write a **synonym** from the list of vocabulary words below on the line. A **synonym** is a word that means the same or nearly the same.

excruciating	exasperate	extortion	extraneous	exultation
extemporaneous	existence	expenditure	excise	

1. triumph _____
2. offhand _____
3. life _____
4. unimportant _____
5. expense _____
6. blackmail _____
7. annoy _____
8. remove _____
9. painful _____

> **Did You Know?** The prefix *ex-* is frequently used in our language. It means "out."
> Some words using this prefix are *excel, exalt, exceed, exhaust,* and *exit.*

Directions: Write an **antonym** from the list of vocabulary words below on the line. An **antonym** is a word that means the opposite or nearly opposite.

expound	exorbitant	exalt	exonerate	explicit
extract	exuberant	exert	exquisite	

1. vague _____
2. penetrate _____
3. condemn _____
4. waste _____
5. degrade _____
6. unattractive _____
7. reasonable _____
8. depressed _____
9. baffle _____

Directions: Write a sentence for each of the vocabulary words below on your own paper. Remember to check your spelling and punctuation.

exhort   **extremity**

Extend Your Vocabulary

1. Survey 25 people about what they think is exquisite. Categorize the information, chart it, and share it with your class.
2. Write explicit directions on how to make something. Then have another person make it.
3. Expound on a topic such as "the hazards of smoking." Write a persuasive piece.
4. Write a narrative piece about a time when you were exuberant.

Name: _____   Date: _____

Unit 24: "X" (Ex) Words: *Vocabulary Quiz*

Directions: Match each vocabulary word with the correct meaning. Write the word on the line next to the meaning.

expenditure	**existence**	**exquisite**	**extract**	**exert**
exasperate	**extremity**	**exuberant**	**exultation**	**exalt**
excruciating	**explicit**	**exonerate**	**extraneous**	**exhort**
extemporaneous	**extortion**	**exorbitant**	**expound**	**excise**

1. _____ obtaining by threats, force, fraud, or wrong use of authority

2. _____ put into use; use fully

3. _____ free from blame

4. _____ an exulting; great rejoicing

5. _____ make high in rank, honor, power, character, or quality; praise; glorify

6. _____ pull out or draw out, usually with some effort

7. _____ not essential

8. _____ spoken or done without preparation

9. _____ causing great suffering

10. _____ very lovely; delicate; most admirable

11. _____ cut out

12. _____ being; a being real

13. _____ urge strongly; advise or warn earnestly

14. _____ using up; a spending

15. _____ much too high; unreasonably excessive

16. _____ the very end; farthest possible place; last point or part

17. _____ make clear; explain

18. _____ irritate very much; annoy greatly; make angry

19. _____ abounding in health and high spirits; overflowing with good cheer

20. _____ clearly expressed; definite

96

Name: _____   Date: _____

Unit 25: "Y" and "Z" Words: *Vocabulary List and Alphabetizing*

Zany
Yucca
Zealot
Yaws

yelp (yelp)   yeoman (yō´ mən)

yonder (yon´ dər)   yore (yôr)

yowl (youl)   yucca (yuk´ ə)

Yule (yōol)   zany (zā´ nē)

yew (yōo)   yesteryear (yes´ tər yir´)

yen (yen)   zwieback (swī´ bak)

yearling (yir´ ling)   yawl (yôl)

zither (zith´ ər)   zealot (zel´ ət)

yaws (yôz)   yarrow (yar´ ō)

zephyr (zef´ ər)   yachtsman (yots´ mən)

Directions: Write the above vocabulary words in alphabetical order below.

1. _____   11. _____

2. _____   12. _____

3. _____   13. _____

4. _____   14. _____

5. _____   15. _____

6. _____   16. _____

7. _____   17. _____

8. _____   18. _____

9. _____   19. _____

10. _____   20. _____

Unit 25: "Y" and "Z" Words: *Get the Facts!*

yelp (yelp) the quick, sharp bark or cry of a dog, fox, etc. *The dog's yelp could be heard down the block.*

yeoman (yō´ mən) naval petty officer who performs clerical duties. *The yeoman's clerical skills were invaluable to his superior officer.*

yonder (yon´ dər) within sight but not near; over there. *I see him out yonder among the trees.*

yore (yôr) long since gone. *He told us a story about knights of yore.*

yowl (youl) long, distressful or dismal cry. *The yowl of the dog worried me.*

yucca (yuk´ ə) plant found in dry, warm regions of North and Central America having stiff, narrow leaves at the base and an upright cluster of bell-shaped flowers. *The landscape architect uses yucca plants in the designs for his clients' yards.*

Yule (yōol) Yuletide; Christmas. *At Yule, many traditions are practiced in our house.*

zany (zā´ nē) clownish; idiotic. *The zany actor had the audience laughing hysterically.*

yew (yōo) evergreen tree native to Europe and Asia. *We put colored lights on our yews last Christmas.*

yesteryear (yes´ tər yir´) last year; the year before this; in past years. *Yesteryear was special because I got married.*

yen (yen) unit of money in Japan. *How much is a yen worth in our currency?*

zwieback (swī´ bak) kind of bread or cake cut into slices and toasted dry in an oven. *Babies like to chew on zwieback when they are teething.*

yearling (yir´ ling) one year old. *She has a yearling colt on her farm.*

yawl (yôl) boat with a large mast near the bow and a small mast near the stern. *I sailed on the tranquil water on a yawl.*

zither (zith´ ər) musical instrument having 30 to 40 strings, played with the fingers and a plectrum. *She played a zither at the Folk Art Festival.*

zealot (zel´ ət) person who shows too much zeal. *He was a zealot about the world coming to an end.*

yaws (yôz) contagious disease of the tropics that produces sores on the skin. *I contracted yaws while vacationing in the tropics.*

yarrow (yar´ ō) a common plant with finely divided leaves and flat clusters of white or pink flowers. *There was some yarrow growing in the backyard.*

zephyr (zef´ ər) the west wind; strong, gentle breeze. *The zephyr was a welcome addition to the hot day.*

yachtsman (yots´ mən) person who owns or sails a yacht. *The yachtsman takes people out for a leisurely ride on his yacht.*

Name: _____ Date: _____

Unit 25: "Y" and "Z" Words: *Skills and Practice*

Directions: Write a **synonym** from the list of vocabulary words below on the line. A **synonym** is a word that means the same or nearly the same.

yew	yore	yelp	yesteryear	zany
yawl	yowl	zealot	Yule	zephyr

1. Christmas _____
2. last year _____
3. fanatic _____
4. bark _____
5. long past _____
6. howl _____
7. evergreen _____
8. foolish _____
9. boat _____
10. breeze _____

> **Did You Know?** *Zwieback* is from German *zwieback,* meaning a "biscuit," which comes from *zwie,* meaning "twice," and *backen,* meaning "to bake."

Directions: Use the vocabulary words below to give an example(s) for each category. Write the word(s) on the line.

yaws	yen	zither	yucca	zwieback	yarrow

1. money _____
2. plant _____
3. disease _____
4. instrument _____
5. toasted bread _____

Directions: Write a sentence for each of the vocabulary words below on your own paper. Remember to check for spelling and punctuation.

yeoman	yonder	yachtsman	yearling

Extend Your Vocabulary

1. List as many careers as you can that deal with the sea, such as yeoman and yachtsman.
2. Create a list of traditions you have at Yuletide. Compare with a friend.
3. Make a T-chart. Name plants or trees and their locations. For example: *yew - Europe, Asia* and *yucca - North and Central America.*
4. Write a narrative piece about a time when you were zany. Include where you were, who you were with, what happened, why it was zany, and how you felt.

Name: _____   Date: _____

Unit 25: "Y" and "Z" Words: *Vocabulary Quiz*

Directions: Match each vocabulary word with the correct meaning. Write the word on the line next to the meaning.

yachtsman	**yelp**	**yeoman**	**yonder**	**yore**
yesteryear	**yowl**	**yucca**	**yarrow**	**Yule**
yearling	**yew**	**yawl**	**yaws**	**yen**
zwieback	**zany**	**zealot**	**zither**	**zephyr**

1. _____ common plant with finely divided leaves and flat clusters of white or pink flowers

2. _____ quick, sharp bark or cry of a dog, fox, etc.

3. _____ contagious disease of the tropics that produces sores on the skin

4. _____ long since gone

5. _____ person who owns or sails a yacht

6. _____ Yuletide; Christmas

7. _____ person who shows too much zeal

8. _____ unit of money in Japan

9. _____ kind of bread or cake cut into slices and toasted dry in an oven

10. _____ evergreen tree native to Europe and Asia

11. _____ clownish, idiotic

12. _____ long, distressful or dismal cry

13. _____ musical instrument having 30 or 40 strings, played with the fingers and a plectrum

14. _____ within sight but not near; over there

15. _____ the west wind; strong, gentle breeze

16. _____ plant found in dry, warm regions of North and Central America having stiff, narrow leaves at the base and an upright cluster of bell-shaped flowers

17. _____ boat with a large mast near the bow and a small mast near the stern

18. _____ last year; the year before this; in past years

19. _____ one year old

20. _____ naval petty officer who performs clerical duties

100

Additional Vocabulary Words

abdicate
acquit
adamant
adhere
aesthetic
affidavit
affirmative
agrarian
alimony
allotment
amenable
amity
antediluvian
antidote
arable
armament
askew
asphyxiation
audacity
avert

barracks
barricade
beau
beguile
benediction
beneficial
bequeath
bewilder
billiards
blare
bliss
brave
buoyancy

cache
canine
cantankerous
caste
caucus
chassis
collateral
concentric
condone

constraint
contortion
convene
corrode
countenance
curtail
cynical

debase
debutante
decipher
delusion
denomination
derivative
desirous
destitute
detonate
dexterity
diffuse
dilapidated
diligent
disengage
dissuade
divert
dredge
dubious

edible
elope
eloquent
embankment
embargo
ember
emphasize
enact
endow
endurance
enliven
escapade
essential
evasive
expend
exterminate

facsimile
farce
faulty
feasible
feint
filtration
flagrant
flippant
flounder
foresight
fortitude
foundry
foyer
frenzy
furlough

gala
galleon
gape
garnish
garrison
gaseous
gauge
generalize
girder
glint
gore
gradation
granulate
grim
grope
guinea

hallowed
hardy
harmonize
haven
hearse
heave
hectic
hence
heresy
heretic

heron
horde
hospitable
hover
humiliate
hybrid
hydraulic

idle
idolize
illogical
impeach
impersonate
incandescent
incense
inclusive
incompetent
incriminate
indebted
informant
initial
initiation
ink
inlaid
inquisition
insignia
insolent
insurrection
integrate
interrogate
intuition
inverse
invert
itemize

jaundice
judicious
junior
justifiable
juvenile

Additional Vocabulary Words (cont.)

kaiser	obstinate	quackery	wadi
keratin	obstruct	quake	warmonger
ketch	occupant	quasar	warren
kindle	officiate	quibble	watermark
kingpin	oratory	quinine	wholesome
knead	ordain		
knurl	ordinance	recoil	xebec
	orthodox	regal	xenophobia
lapse	outgrowth	renown	xylem
lateral	outskirts	resolute	
latter	overcast	rite	yammer
legacy			yoga
legation	pacifist	saga	yuan
liability	paraphrase	sardonic	yurt
livelihood	parish	sentinel	
lore	paternal	sever	zaftig
lull	pauper	sham	zeal
lustrous	pensive	stupor	zenith
	perennial	succumb	zeppelin
mainstay	perforate		zodiac
mallet	perjury	temperance	
maritime	perseverance	theorem	
mason	perturb	thorax	
maul	physique	trapeze	
meritorious	piety	trivial	
mirage	pigment		
momentary	pious	ultrasound	
monologue	placard	umber	
municipal	posterior	urchin	
mute	potent	usage	
mutilate	predecessor	utilize	
	prodigy	utopia	
nautical	prospectus		
navigable	prudent	valor	
neuter	purge	vapid	
noncommittal	putrid	variegated	
nonexistent		vice	
noteworthy		visualize	
nourish		voucher	

Name: _____ Date: _____

Compare and Contrast T-Chart

_____
(Chart Title)

(Item being compared)	(Item being compared)
_____	_____
_____	_____
_____	_____
_____	_____
_____	_____
_____	_____
_____	_____
_____	_____
_____	_____
_____	_____
_____	_____
_____	_____
_____	_____

* Use with Extend Your Vocabulary activities asking for a T-chart to compare and contrast two things.

Name: _____ Date: _____

List Activity

_____
(Title of List)

_____   _____   _____

_____   _____   _____

_____   _____   _____

_____   _____   _____

_____   _____   _____

_____   _____   _____

_____   _____   _____

_____   _____   _____

_____   _____   _____

_____   _____   _____

_____   _____   _____

_____   _____   _____

_____   _____   _____

_____   _____   _____

_____   _____   _____

* Use with Extend Your Vocabulary activities asking for a list of things.

Name: _____   Date: _____

Venn Diagram

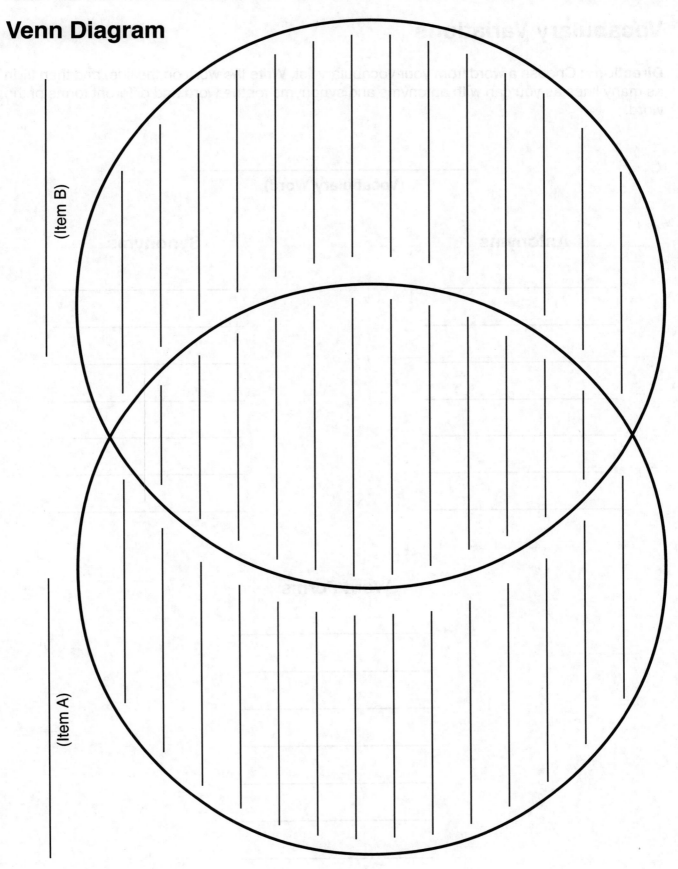

Name: _____ Date: _____

Vocabulary Variations

Directions: Choose a word from your vocabulary list. Write the word on the line, and then fill in as many lines as you can with antonyms and synonyms for the word and different forms of the word.

_____
(Vocabulary Word)

Antonyms

_____

_____

_____

_____

_____

_____

_____

Synonyms

_____

_____

_____

_____

_____

_____

Word Forms

_____

_____

_____

_____

_____

_____

Name: _____ Date: _____

Word Web

Directions: Choose a word from your vocabulary list. Write the word in the center. Fill in the rest of the word web.

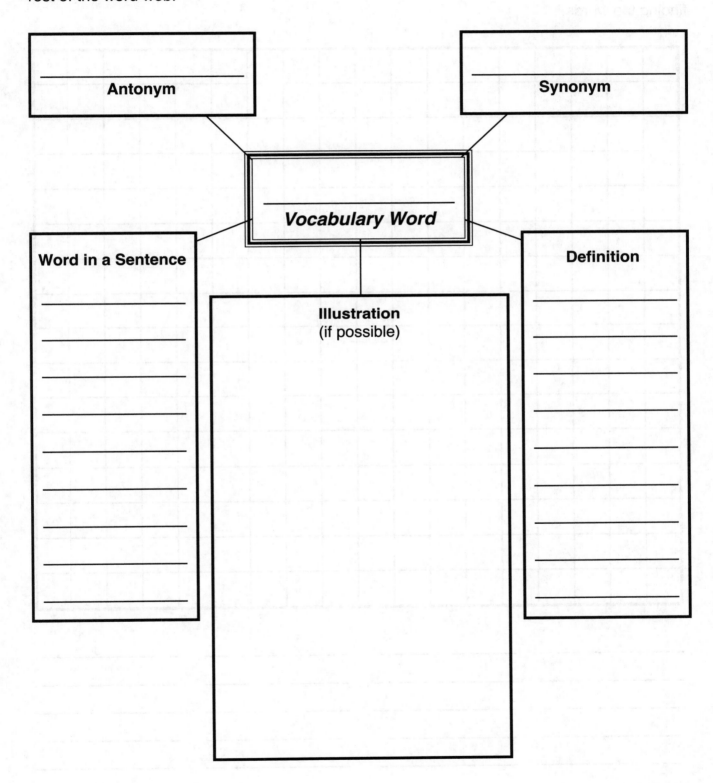

Name: _____ Date: _____

Word Search

Directions: Use your vocabulary words to make your own word search. Give it to a partner to try when you are finished. Write the list of words below the puzzle for your partner to use when finding the words.

Author Time!

Directions: Compose a writing piece using as many words from your vocabulary list as you can. Keep in mind your list of words and the many types of writing you could do, such as persuasive, expository, or narrative. Use extra paper if you need it.

List your vocabulary words. Place an X by the ones you use in your writing piece.

_____   _____   _____   _____
_____   _____   _____   _____
_____   _____   _____   _____
_____   _____   _____   _____
_____   _____   _____   _____

Writing piece:

_____
_____
_____
_____
_____
_____
_____
_____
_____
_____
_____
_____
_____

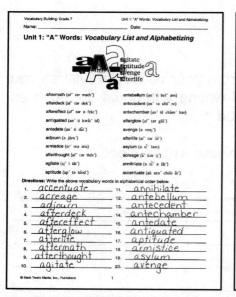

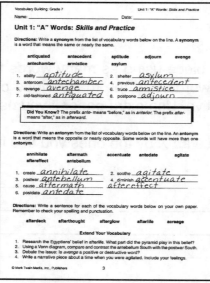

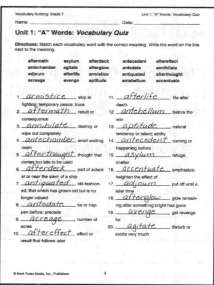

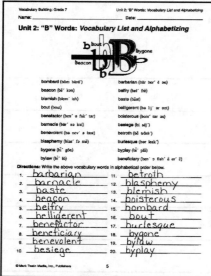

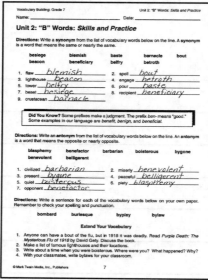

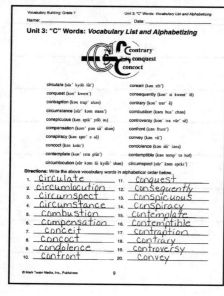

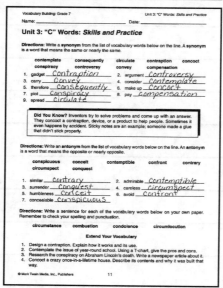

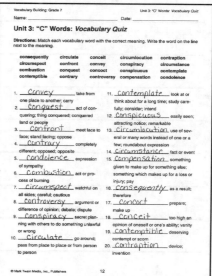

Vocabulary Building: Grade 7 — Unit 4: "D" Words: *Vocabulary List and Alphabetizing*

Name: ______________ Date: ______________

Unit 4: "D" Words: *Vocabulary List and Alphabetizing*

discourse (dis´ kôrs´)	disposition (dis´ pə zish´ ən)
defiance (di fī´ əns)	demerit (di mer´ it)
devise (di vīs´)	distinction (di stingk´ shən)
disband (dis band´)	discord (dis´ kôrd´)
disregard (dis´ ri gärd´)	debris (də brē´)
disintegrate (dis in´ tə grāt´)	dispensary (di spen´ sə rē)
distort (di stôrt´)	demure (di myŏŏr´)
discretion (di skresh´ ən)	dishevel (di shev´ əl)
disreputable (dis rep´ yōō tə bəl)	decrepit (di krep´ it)
deplete (di plēt´)	disperse (di spûrs´)

Directions: Write the above vocabulary words in alphabetical order below.

1. debris 11. discretion
2. decrepit 12. dishevel
3. defiance 13. disintegrate
4. demerit 14. dispensary
5. demure 15. disperse
6. deplete 16. disposition
7. devise 17. disregard
8. disband 18. disreputable
9. discord 19. distinction
10. discourse 20. distort

© Mark Twain Media, Inc., Publishers 13

Vocabulary Building: Grade 7 — Unit 4: "D" Words: *Skills and Practice*

Name: ______________ Date: ______________

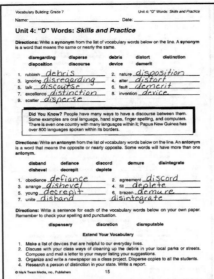

Unit 4: "D" Words: *Skills and Practice*

Directions: Write a **synonym** from the list of vocabulary words below on the line. A **synonym** is a word that means the same or nearly the same.

disregarding disperse debris distort distinction disposition discourse device demerit

1. rubbish debris 2. nature disposition
3. ignoring disregarding 4. alter distort
5. talk discourse 6. fault demerit
7. excellence distinction 8. invention device
9. scatter disperse

Did You Know? People have many ways to have a discourse between them. Some examples are oral language, hand signs, finger spelling, and computers. There is even one country with many languages within it; Papua New Guinea has over 800 languages spoken within its borders.

Directions: Write an **antonym** from the list of vocabulary words below on the line. An **antonym** is a word that means the opposite or nearly opposite. Some words will have more than one antonym.

disband defiance discord demure disintegrate dishevel decrepit deplete

1. obedience defiance 2. agreement discord
3. arrange dishevel 4. fill deplete
5. young decrepit 6. brazen demure
7. unite disband disintegrate

Directions: Write a sentence for each of the vocabulary words below on your own paper. Remember to check your spelling and punctuation.

dispensary discretion disreputable

Extend Your Vocabulary

1. Make a list of devices that are helpful to our everyday lives.
2. Discuss with your class ways of cleaning up the debris in your local parks or streets. Compose and mail a letter to your mayor listing your suggestions.
3. Organize and write a newspaper as a class project. Disperse copies to all the students.
4. Research a person of distinction in your state. Write a report.

© Mark Twain Media, Inc., Publishers 15

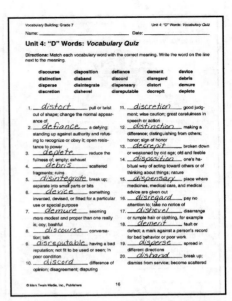

Vocabulary Building: Grade 7 — Unit 4: "D" Words: *Vocabulary Quiz*

Name: ______________ Date: ______________

Unit 4: "D" Words: *Vocabulary Quiz*

Directions: Match each vocabulary word with the correct meaning. Write the word on the line next to the meaning.

discourse	disposition	defiance	demerit	device
distinction	disband	discord	disregard	debris
disperse	disintegrate	dispensary	distort	demure
discretion	dishevel	disreputable	decrepit	deplete

1. distort pull or twist out of shape; change the normal appearance of
2. defiance a defying; standing up against authority and refusing to recognize or obey it; open resistance to power
3. deplete reduce the fullness of; empty; exhaust
4. debris scattered fragments; ruins
5. disintegrate break up; separate into small parts or bits
6. device something invented, devised, or fitted for a particular use or special purpose
7. demure seeming more modest and proper than one really is; coy; bashful
8. discourse conversation; talk
9. disreputable having a bad reputation; not fit to be used or seen; in poor condition
10. discord difference of opinion; disagreement; disputing
11. discretion good judgment; wise caution; great carefulness in speech or action
12. distinction making a difference; distinguishing from others; honor; sign of honor
13. decrepit broken down or weakened by old age; old and feeble
14. disposition one's habitual way of acting toward others or of thinking about things; nature
15. dispensary place where medicines, medical care, and medical advice are given out
16. disregard pay no attention to; take no notice of
17. dishevel disarrange or rumple hair or clothing, for example
18. demerit fault or defect; a mark against a person's record for bad behavior or poor work
19. disperse spread in different directions
20. disband break up; dismiss from service; become scattered

© Mark Twain Media, Inc., Publishers 16

Vocabulary Building: Grade 7 — Unit 5: "E" Words: *Vocabulary List and Alphabetizing*

Name: ______________ Date: ______________

Unit 5: "E" Words: *Vocabulary List and Alphabetizing*

enterprise (ent´ ər prīz´)	epicenter (ep´ i sent´ ər)
embezzle (em bez´ əl)	eccentric (ak sen´ trik)
epicure (ep´ i kyŏŏr´)	elongate (i lông´ gāt´)
elude (i lōōd´)	epidemic (ep´ ə dem´ ik)
eradicate (i rad´ ə kāt)	espionage (es´ pē ə näzh´)
epidermis (ep´ ə dûr´ mis)	entice (en tīs´)
effigy (ef´ i jē)	epigram (ep´ ə gram´)
embroil (em broil´)	eminent (em´ ə nənt)
epitaph (ep´ ə taf´)	erroneous (ə rō´ nē əs)
encompass (en kum´ pəs)	epitome (i pit´ ə mē´)

Directions: Write the above vocabulary words in alphabetical order below.

1. eccentric 11. epicenter
2. effigy 12. epicure
3. elongate 13. epidemic
4. elude 14. epidermis
5. embezzle 15. epigram
6. embroil 16. epitaph
7. eminent 17. epitome
8. encompass 18. eradicate
9. enterprise 19. erroneous
10. entice 20. espionage

© Mark Twain Media, Inc., Publishers 17

Vocabulary Building: Grade 7 — Unit 5: "E" Words: *Skills and Practice*

Name: ______________ Date: ______________

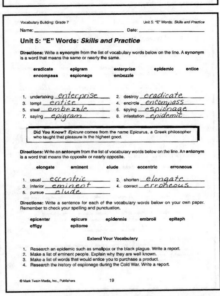

Unit 5: "E" Words: *Skills and Practice*

Directions: Write a **synonym** from the list of vocabulary words below on the line. A **synonym** is a word that means the same or nearly the same.

eradicate epigram enterprise epidemic entice encompass espionage embezzle

1. undertaking enterprise 2. destroy eradicate
3. tempt entice 4. encircle encompass
5. steal embezzle 6. spying espionage
7. saying epigram 8. infestation epidemic

Did You Know? *Epicure* comes from the name Epicurus, a Greek philosopher who taught that pleasure is the highest good.

Directions: Write an **antonym** from the list of vocabulary words below on the line. An **antonym** is a word that means the opposite or nearly opposite.

elongate eminent elude eccentric erroneous

1. usual eccentric 2. shorten elongate
3. inferior eminent 4. correct erroneous
5. pursue elude

Directions: Write a sentence for each of the vocabulary words below on your own paper. Remember to check your spelling and punctuation.

epicenter epicure epidermis embroil epitaph effigy epitome

Extend Your Vocabulary

1. Research an epidemic such as smallpox or the black plague. Write a report.
2. Make a list of eminent people. Explain why they are well known.
3. Make a list of words that would entice you to purchase a product.
4. Research the history of espionage during the Cold War. Write a report.

© Mark Twain Media, Inc., Publishers 19

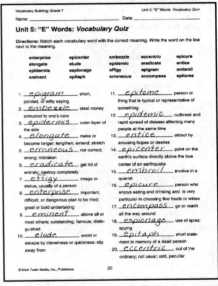

Vocabulary Building: Grade 7 — Unit 5: "E" Words: *Vocabulary Quiz*

Name: ______________ Date: ______________

Unit 5: "E" Words: *Vocabulary Quiz*

Directions: Match each vocabulary word with the correct meaning. Write the word on the line next to the meaning.

enterprise	epicenter	embezzle	eccentric	epicure
elongate	elude	epidemic	eradicate	entice
epidermis	espionage	effigy	epigram	embroil
eminent	epitaph	erroneous	encompass	epitome

1. epigram short, pointed, or witty saying
2. embezzle steal money entrusted to one's care
3. epidermis outer layer of the skin
4. elongate make or become longer; lengthen; extend; stretch
5. erroneous not correct; wrong; mistaken
6. eradicate get rid of entirely; destroy completely
7. effigy image or statue, usually of a person
8. enterprise important, difficult, or dangerous plan to be tried; great or bold undertaking
9. eminent above all or most others; outstanding; famous; distinguished
10. elude avoid or escape by cleverness or quickness; slip away from
11. epitome person or thing that is typical or representative of something
12. epidemic outbreak and rapid spread of disease affecting many people at the same time
13. entice attract by arousing hopes or desires
14. epicenter point on the earth's surface directly above the true center of an earthquake
15. embroil involve in a quarrel
16. epicure person who enjoys eating and drinking and is very particular in choosing fine foods or wines
17. encompass go or reach all the way around
18. espionage use of spies; spying
19. epitaph short statement in memory of a dead person
20. eccentric out of the ordinary; not usual; odd, peculiar

© Mark Twain Media, Inc., Publishers 20

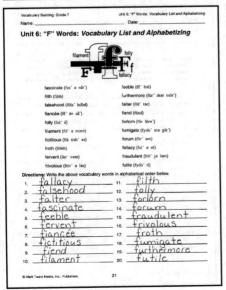

Vocabulary Building: Grade 7 — Unit 6: "F" Words: *Vocabulary List and Alphabetizing*

Name: ______________ Date: ______________

Unit 6: "F" Words: *Vocabulary List and Alphabetizing*

fascinate (fas´ ə nāt´)	feeble (fē´ bəl)
filth (filth)	furthermore (fûr´ *th*ər môr´)
falsehood (fôls´ hŏŏd)	falter (fôl´ tər)
fiancée (fē´ än sā´)	fiend (fēnd)
folly (fol´ ē)	forlorn (fôr lôrn´)
filament (fil´ ə mənt)	fumigate (fyōō´ mə gāt´)
fictitious (fik tish´ əs)	forum (fôr´ əm)
froth (frôth)	fallacy (fal´ ə sē)
fervent (fer´ vənt)	fraudulent (frô´ jə lənt)
frivolous (friv´ ə ləs)	futile (fyōō´ tl)

Directions: Write the above vocabulary words in alphabetical order below.

1. fallacy 11. filth
2. falsehood 12. folly
3. falter 13. forlorn
4. fascinate 14. forum
5. feeble 15. fraudulent
6. fervent 16. frivolous
7. fiancée 17. froth
8. fictitious 18. fumigate
9. fiend 19. furthermore
10. filament 20. futile

© Mark Twain Media, Inc., Publishers 21

Vocabulary Building: Grade 7 — Unit 6: "F" Words: *Skills and Practice*

Name: ______________ Date: ______________

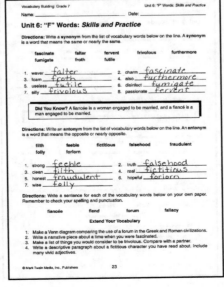

Unit 6: "F" Words: *Skills and Practice*

Directions: Write a **synonym** from the list of vocabulary words below on the line. A **synonym** is a word that means the same or nearly the same.

fascinate falter fervent frivolous furthermore fumigate froth futile

1. waver falter 2. charm fascinate
3. foam froth 4. also furthermore
5. useless futile 6. disinfect fumigate
7. silly frivolous 8. passionate fervent

Did You Know? A fiancée is a woman engaged to be married, and a fiancé is a man engaged to be married.

Directions: Write an **antonym** from the list of vocabulary words below on the line. An **antonym** is a word that means the opposite or nearly opposite.

filth feeble fictitious falsehood fraudulent folly forlorn

1. strong feeble 2. truth falsehood
3. clean filth 4. real fictitious
5. honest fraudulent 6. hopeful forlorn
7. wise folly

Directions: Write a sentence for each of the vocabulary words below on your own paper. Remember to check your spelling and punctuation.

fiancée fiend forum fallacy

Extend Your Vocabulary

1. Make a Venn diagram comparing the use of a forum in the Greek and Roman civilizations.
2. Write a narrative piece about a time when you were fascinated.
3. Make a list of things you would consider to be frivolous. Compare with a partner.
4. Write a descriptive paragraph about a fictitious character you have read about. Include many vivid adjectives.

© Mark Twain Media, Inc., Publishers 23

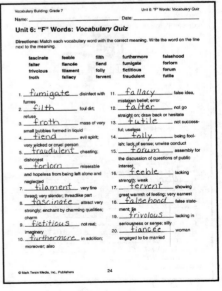

Vocabulary Building: Grade 7 — Unit 6: "F" Words: *Vocabulary Quiz*

Name: ______________ Date: ______________

Unit 6: "F" Words: *Vocabulary Quiz*

Directions: Match each vocabulary word with the correct meaning. Write the word on the line next to the meaning.

fascinate	feeble	filth	furthermore	falsehood
falter	fiancée	fiend	fumigate	forlorn
frivolous	filament	folly	fictitious	forum
froth	fallacy	fervent	fraudulent	futile

1. fumigate disinfect with fumes
2. filth foul dirt; refuse
3. froth mass of very small bubbles formed in liquid
4. fiend evil spirit; very wicked or cruel person
5. fraudulent cheating; dishonest
6. forlorn miserable and hopeless from being left alone and neglected
7. filament very fine thread; very slender; threadlike part
8. fascinate attract very strongly; enchant by charming qualities; charm
9. fictitious not real; imaginary
10. furthermore in addition; moreover; also
11. fallacy false idea, mistaken belief; error
12. falter not go straight on; draw back or hesitate
13. futile not successful; useless
14. folly being foolish; lack of sense; unwise conduct
15. forum assembly for the discussion of questions of public interest
16. feeble lacking strength; weak
17. fervent showing great warmth of feeling; very earnest
18. falsehood false statement; lie
19. frivolous lacking in seriousness or sense; silly
20. fiancée woman engaged to be married

© Mark Twain Media, Inc., Publishers 24

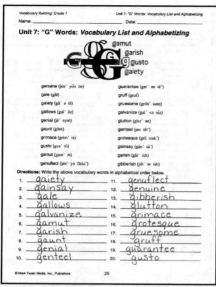

Vocabulary Building: Grade 7 — Unit 7: "G" Words: *Vocabulary List and Alphabetizing*

Name: ____________ Date: ____________

Unit 7: "G" Words: *Vocabulary List and Alphabetizing*

genuine (jen´ yōō ən)	guarantee (gar´ ən tē´)
gale (gāl)	gruff (gruf)
gaiety (gā´ ə tē)	gruesome (grōō´ səm)
gallows (gal´ ōz)	galvanize (gal´ və nīz)
genial (jē´ nyəl)	glutton (glut´ ən)
gaunt (gônt)	genteel (jen tēl´)
grimace (grim´ is)	grotesque (grō tesk´)
gusto (gus´ tō)	gainsay (gān´ sā´)
gamut (gam´ ət)	garish (gâr´ ish)
genuflect (jen´ yə flekt´)	gibberish (jib´ ər ish)

Directions: Write the above vocabulary words in alphabetical order below.

1. gaiety
2. gainsay
3. gale
4. gallows
5. galvanize
6. gamut
7. garish
8. gaunt
9. genial
10. genteel
11. genuflect
12. genuine
13. gibberish
14. glutton
15. grimace
16. grotesque
17. gruesome
18. gruff
19. guarantee
20. gusto

© Mark Twain Media, Inc., Publishers 25

Vocabulary Building: Grade 7 — Unit 7: "G" Words: *Skills and Practice*

Name: ____________ Date: ____________

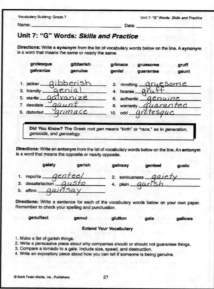

Unit 7: "G" Words: *Skills and Practice*

Directions: Write a **synonym** from the list of vocabulary words below on the line. A **synonym** is a word that means the same or nearly the same.

grotesque **gibberish** **grimace** **gruesome** **gruff**
galvanize **genuine** **genial** **guarantee** **gaunt**

1. jabber gibberish
2. revolting gruesome
3. friendly genial
4. hoarse gruff
5. startle galvanize
6. authentic genuine
7. desolate gaunt
8. warranty guarantee
9. distorted grimace
10. odd grotesque

Did You Know? The Greek root *gen* means "birth" or "race," as in *generation, genocide,* and *genealogy.*

Directions: Write an **antonym** from the list of vocabulary words below on the line. An **antonym** is a word that means the opposite or nearly opposite.

gaiety **garish** **gainsay** **genteel** **gusto**

1. impolite genteel
2. seriousness gaiety
3. dissatisfaction gusto
4. plain garish
5. affirm gainsay

Directions: Write a sentence for each of the vocabulary words below on your own paper. Remember to check your spelling and punctuation.

genuflect **gamut** **glutton** **gale** **gallows**

Extend Your Vocabulary

1. Make a list of garish things.
2. Write a persuasive piece about why companies should or should not guarantee things.
3. Compare a tornado to a gale. Include size, speed, and destruction.
4. Write an expository piece about how you can tell if someone is being genuine.

© Mark Twain Media, Inc., Publishers 27

Vocabulary Building: Grade 7 — Unit 7: "G" Words: *Vocabulary Quiz*

Name: ____________ Date: ____________

Unit 7: "G" Words: *Vocabulary Quiz*

Directions: Match each vocabulary word with the correct meaning. Write the word on the line next to the meaning.

genuine	**guarantee**	**grotesque**	**gruff**	**gaiety**
gruesome	**gallows**	**galvanize**	**genial**	**glutton**
gibberish	**genteel**	**grimace**	**gale**	**gusto**
gainsay	**genuflect**	**garish**	**gamut**	**gaunt**

1. genuine actually being what it seems or is claimed to be; real; sincere
2. gainsay deny; contradict; dispute
3. gallows wooden frame constructed of a crossbar on two upright posts, used for hanging
4. gibberish senseless chatter; confused, meaningless talk or writing
5. gaiety cheerful liveliness; joyousness
6. grimace twisting or distortion of the face; ugly or funny smile
7. genteel polite; well-bred; fashionable; elegant
8. gusto hearty enjoyment
9. gale very strong wind
10. grotesque odd or unnatural in shape, appearance, or manner; odd
11. gruesome causing fear or horror; horrible; revolting
12. genuflect bend the knee as an act of reverence or worship
13. glutton person who never seems to have enough of something
14. gamut whole range of anything
15. guarantee promise or pledge to replace or repair a purchased product or to return the money paid, if unsatisfactory
16. garish unpleasantly bright; glaring; gaudy
17. gruff deep and harsh; hoarse
18. gaunt pinched and lean; harsh or forlorn in appearance
19. genial smiling and pleasant; cheerful and friendly
20. galvanize to stimulate as if by electric shock; startle; to plate with zinc

© Mark Twain Media, Inc., Publishers 28

Vocabulary Building: Grade 7 — Unit 8: "H" Words: *Vocabulary List and Alphabetizing*

Name: ____________ Date: ____________

Unit 8: "H" Words: *Vocabulary List and Alphabetizing*

horticulture (hôr´ tə kul´ chər)	humane (hyōō mān´)
haughty (hôt´ ē)	hoard (hôrd)
heirloom (er´ lōōm)	hideous (hid´ ē əs)
homage (hom´ ij)	hypocrite (hip´ ə krit)
hysteria (hi ster´ ē ə)	hallucination (hə lōō´ si nā´ shən)
haphazard (hap´ haz´ ərd)	herbivorous (hər biv´ ər əs)
hindrance (hin´ drəns)	hypertension (hī´ pər ten´ shən)
hypertrophy (hī pûr´ trə fē)	hypochondria (hī´ pə kon´ drē ə)
hypotenuse (hī pot´ 'n ōōs´)	hypodermic (hī´ pə dûr´ mik)
hypothesis (hī poth´ ə sis)	hypoglycemia (hī´ pō glī sē´ mē ə)

Directions: Write the above vocabulary words in alphabetical order below.

1. hallucination
2. haphazard
3. haughty
4. heirloom
5. herbivorous
6. hideous
7. hindrance
8. hoard
9. homage
10. homicide
11. humane
12. hypertension
13. hypertrophy
14. hypochondria
15. hypocrite
16. hypodermic
17. hypoglycemia
18. hypotenuse
19. hypothesis
20. hysteria

© Mark Twain Media, Inc., Publishers 29

Vocabulary Building: Grade 7 — Unit 8: "H" Words: *Skills and Practice*

Name: ____________ Date: ____________

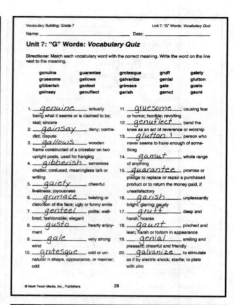

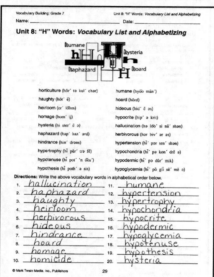

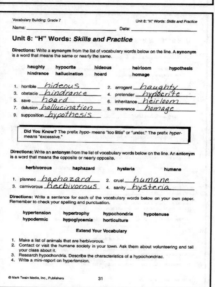

Unit 8: "H" Words: *Skills and Practice*

Directions: Write a **synonym** from the list of vocabulary words below on the line. A **synonym** is a word that means the same or nearly the same.

haughty **hypocrite** **hideous** **heirloom** **hypothesis**
hindrance **hallucination** **hoard** **homage**

1. horrible hideous
2. arrogant haughty
3. obstacle hindrance
4. pretender hypocrite
5. save hoard
6. inheritance heirloom
7. delusion hallucination
8. reverence homage
9. supposition hypothesis

Did You Know? The prefix *hypo-* means "too little" or "under." The prefix *hyper-* means "excessive."

Directions: Write an **antonym** from the list of vocabulary words below on the line. An **antonym** is a word that means the opposite or nearly opposite.

herbivorous **haphazard** **hysteria** **humane**

1. planned haphazard
2. cruel humane
3. carnivorous herbivorous
4. sanity hysteria

Directions: Write a sentence for each of the vocabulary words below on your own paper. Remember to check your spelling and punctuation.

hypertension **hypertrophy** **hypochondria** **hypotenuse**
hypodermic **hypoglycemia** **horticulture**

Extend Your Vocabulary

1. Make a list of animals that are herbivorous.
2. Contact or visit the humane society in your town. Ask them about volunteering and tell your class about it.
3. Research hypochondria. Describe the characteristics of a hypochondriac.
4. Write a mini-report on hypertension.

© Mark Twain Media, Inc., Publishers 31

Vocabulary Building: Grade 7 — Unit 8: "H" Words: *Vocabulary Quiz*

Name: ____________ Date: ____________

Unit 8: "H" Words: *Vocabulary Quiz*

Directions: Match each vocabulary word with the correct meaning. Write the word on the line next to the meaning.

horticulture	**humane**	**haughty**	**herbivorous**	**heirloom**
hypodermic	**homage**	**hypocrite**	**hypotenuse**	**hallucination**
haphazard	**hoard**	**hindrance**	**hypertension**	**hypertrophy**
hypochondria	**hysteria**	**hideous**	**hypothesis**	**hypoglycemia**

1. hindrance person or thing that hinders; obstacle
2. humane not cruel or brutal; kind; merciful
3. hypothesis something assumed because it seems likely to be a true explanation; theory
4. hallucination seeing or hearing things that exist only in a person's imagination
5. herbivorous feeding on grass or other plants
6. horticulture art or science of growing flowers, fruits, vegetable, or shrubs, especially in a garden or orchard
7. hypertension an abnormally high blood pressure
8. hideous very ugly; frightful; horrible
9. hypochondria abnormal anxiety over one's health; imaginary illness
10. hypocrite person who is not sincere; pretender
11. hypodermic under the skin
12. haphazard not planned; random
13. hypertrophy enlargement of a body part or organ
14. hoard save and store away
15. hypoglycemia condition caused by a lowered level of sugar in the blood, usually because of the presence of too much insulin
16. heirloom possession handed down from generation to generation
17. hypotenuse the side of a right triangle opposite the right angle
18. hysteria mental illness caused by anxiety or worry
19. haughty too proud of oneself and too scornful of others
20. homage dutiful respect; reverence; honor

© Mark Twain Media, Inc., Publishers 32

Vocabulary Building: Grade 7 — Unit 9: "I" Words: *Vocabulary List and Alphabetizing*

Name: ____________ Date: ____________

Unit 9: "I" Words: *Vocabulary List and Alphabetizing*

immense (i mens´)	impose (im pōz´)
inflammable (in flam´ ə bəl)	infuriate (in fyōōr´ ē āt)
intrigue (in trēg´)	indelible (in del´ ə bəl)
infantry (in´ fən trē)	instantaneous (in´ stən tā´ nē əs)
illustrious (i lus´ trē əs)	impertinent (im pûrt´ 'n ənt)
innumerable (in nōō´ mer ə bəl)	inclination (in´ klə nā´ shən)
instigate (in´ stə gāt´)	inevitable (in ev´ i tə bəl)
illiterate (i lit´ ər it)	immaterial (im´ ə tir´ ē əl)
imperil (im per´ əl)	impudent (im´ pyōō dənt)
insinuate (in sin´ yōō āt´)	indispensable (in´ di spen´ sə bəl)

Directions: Write the above vocabulary words in alphabetical order below.

1. illiterate
2. illustrious
3. immaterial
4. immense
5. imperil
6. impertinent
7. impose
8. impudent
9. inclination
10. indelible
11. indispensable
12. inevitable
13. infantry
14. inflammable
15. infuriate
16. innumerable
17. insinuate
18. instantaneous
19. instigate
20. intrigue

© Mark Twain Media, Inc., Publishers 33

Vocabulary Building: Grade 7 — Unit 9: "I" Words: *Skills and Practice*

Name: ____________ Date: ____________

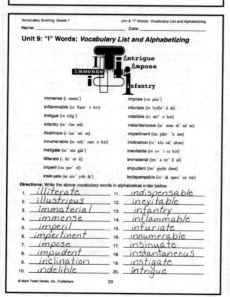

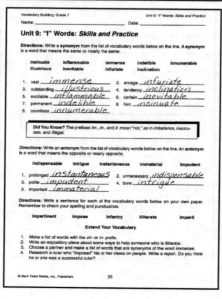

Unit 9: "I" Words: *Skills and Practice*

Directions: Write a **synonym** from the list of vocabulary words below on the line. A **synonym** is a word that means the same or nearly the same.

insinuate **inflammable** **immense** **indelible** **innumerable**
illustrious **inevitable** **infuriate** **inclination**

1. vast immense
2. enrage infuriate
3. outstanding illustrious
4. tendency inclination
5. excitable inflammable
6. certain inevitable
7. permanent indelible
8. hint insinuate
9. countless innumerable

Did You Know? The prefixes *im-*, *in-*, and *il-* mean "not," as in *imbalance, inaccurate,* and *illegal.*

Directions: Write an **antonym** from the list of vocabulary words below on the line. An **antonym** is a word that means the opposite or nearly opposite.

indispensable **intrigue** **instantaneous** **immaterial** **impudent**

1. prolonged instantaneous
2. unnecessary indispensable
3. polite impudent
4. bore intrigue
5. important immaterial

Directions: Write a sentence for each of the vocabulary words below on your own paper. Remember to check your spelling and punctuation.

impertinent **impose** **infantry** **illiterate** **imperil**

Extend Your Vocabulary

1. Make a list of words with the *im-* or *in-* prefix.
2. Write an expository piece about some ways to help someone who is illiterate.
3. Choose a partner and make a list of words that are synonyms of the word *immense.*
4. Research a ruler who "imposed" his or her views on people. Write a report. Do you think he or she was a successful ruler?

© Mark Twain Media, Inc., Publishers 35

Vocabulary Building: Grade 7 — Unit 9: "I" Words: *Vocabulary Quiz*

Name: ____________ Date: ____________

Unit 9: "I" Words: *Vocabulary Quiz*

Directions: Match each vocabulary word with the correct meaning. Write the word on the line next to the meaning.

instantaneous	**impose**	**indelible**	**infuriate**	**intrigue**
inflammable	**infantry**	**immense**	**illustrious**	**impertinent**
indispensable	**inevitable**	**illiterate**	**immaterial**	**imperil**
impudent	**insinuate**	**instigate**	**inclination**	**innumerable**

1. illiterate not knowing how to read and write
2. intrigue excite the curiosity and interest of
3. instigate urge on; stir up
4. instantaneous coming or done in an instant
5. indispensable absolutely necessary
6. immense very large; huge; vast
7. inevitable not to be avoided; sure to happen
8. infuriate fill with wild, fierce anger; make furious
9. insinuate suggest in an indirect way
10. indelible not able to be erased or removed
11. inclination natural bent; tendency
12. illustrious very famous; great; outstanding
13. innumerable cannot be counted; very numerous
14. impertinent not pertinent; not to the point; out of place
15. immaterial not important; insignificant
16. inflammable easily excited or aroused; excitable
17. impudent shamelessly bold; very rude
18. infantry soldiers trained, equipped, and organized to fight on foot
19. imperil put in danger
20. impose force or thrust one's authority or influence on another

© Mark Twain Media, Inc., Publishers 36

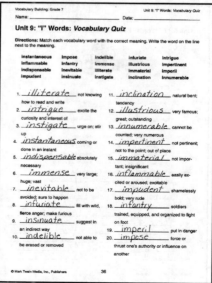

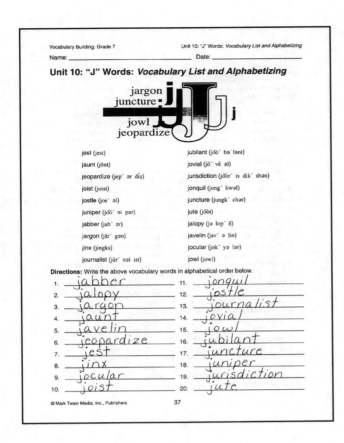

Name: _____ Date: _____

Unit 10: "J" Words: *Vocabulary List and Alphabetizing*

jargon
juncture
jowl
jeopardize

jest (jest)
jaunt (jônt)
jeopardize (jep´ ər dīz)
joist (joist)
jostle (jos´ əl)
juniper (jōō´ ni pər)
jabber (jab´ ər)
jargon (jär´ gən)
jinx (jingks)
journalist (jûr´ nal ist)

jubilant (jōō´ bə lənt)
jovial (jō´ vē əl)
jurisdiction (jōōr´ is dik´ shən)
jonquil (jong´ kwəl)
juncture (jungk´ chər)
jute (jōōt)
jalopy (jə lop´ ē)
javelin (jav´ ə lin)
jocular (jok´ yə lər)
jowl (jowl)

Directions: Write the above vocabulary words in alphabetical order below.

1. jabber
2. jalopy
3. jargon
4. jaunt
5. javelin
6. jeopardize
7. jest
8. jinx
9. jocular
10. joist
11. jonquil
12. jostle
13. journalist
14. jovial
15. jowl
16. jubilant
17. juncture
18. juniper
19. jurisdiction
20. jute

© Mark Twain Media, Inc., Publishers   37

Name: _____ Date: _____

Unit 10: "J" Words: *Skills and Practice*

Directions: Write a **synonym** from the list of vocabulary words below on the line. A **synonym** is a word that means the same or nearly the same.

| jeopardize | jaunt | jowl | jonquil | juncture |
| javelin | jubilant | jest | jalopy | jabber |

1. excursion jaunt
2. joint juncture
3. joke jest
4. imperil jeopardize
5. car jalopy
6. rejoicing jubilant
7. chatter jabber
8. daffodil jonquil
9. jaw jowl
10. spear javelin

> **Did You Know?** The javelin throw started in the original Olympic Games in ancient Greece and is still one of the Olympic sports today.

Directions: Write an **antonym** from the list of vocabulary words below on the line. An **antonym** is a word that means the opposite or nearly opposite.

| jinx | jocular | jovial |

1. wicked jovial
2. four-leaf clover jinx
3. serious jocular

Directions: Write a sentence for each of the vocabulary words below on your own paper. Remember to check your spelling and punctuation.

| jurisdiction | juniper | joist | jostle | jute |
| journalist | jargon |

Extend Your Vocabulary

1. Write a list of words considered as the jargon of a certain profession.
2. Write a persuasive piece on why students should not jeopardize their futures with drugs and alcohol.
3. Interview a local journalist about his or her job. Share the information with your class.
4. Write a narrative piece about a time when your parents used their jurisdiction over you. Include your feelings and why you felt the way you did.

© Mark Twain Media, Inc., Publishers   39

Name: _____ Date: _____

Unit 10: "J" Words: *Vocabulary Quiz*

Directions: Match each vocabulary word with the correct meaning. Write the word on the line next to the meaning.

jest	jubilant	jaunt	jovial	jeopardize
joist	jonquil	jostle	juncture	jurisdiction
jute	jabber	jalopy	jargon	journalist
jinx	jocular	jowl	javelin	juniper

1. jalopy — old automobile in bad condition
2. jeopardize — put in danger; risk; endanger
3. jinx — person or thing believed to bring bad luck
4. jostle — shove, push, or crowd against
5. jabber — talk very fast in a confused, senseless way
6. jest — poke fun; make fun
7. jargon — language of a special group or profession
8. jaunt — a short journey, especially for pleasure
9. jocular — funny; joking
10. joist — one of the parallel beams of timber or steel that supports the boards of a floor or ceiling
11. jowl — jaw, especially the lower jaw
12. juncture — junction; point or line where two things join
13. javelin — lightweight spear thrown by hand
14. jovial — goodhearted and full of fun; good-humored and merry
15. journalist — person whose work is writing for, editing, managing, or publishing a newspaper or magazine
16. jubilant — expressing or showing joy
17. jonquil — plant with yellow or white flowers and long slender leaves
18. jute — strong fiber used for making coarse fabric or rope
19. jurisdiction — right or power to give out justice
20. juniper — evergreen shrub or tree with small, berry-like cones

© Mark Twain Media, Inc., Publishers   40

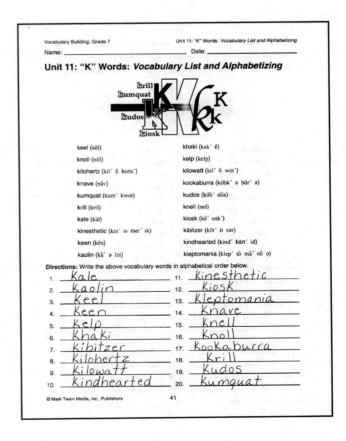

Name: _____ Date: _____

Unit 11: "K" Words: *Vocabulary List and Alphabetizing*

krill
kumquat
kudos
kiosk

keel (kēl)
knoll (nōl)
kilohertz (kil´ ō herts´)
knave (nāv)
kumquat (kum´ kwot)
krill (kril)
kale (kāl)
kinesthetic (kin´ is thet´ ik)
keen (kēn)
kaolin (kā´ ə lin)

khaki (kak´ ē)
kelp (kelp)
kilowatt (kil´ ō wot´)
kookaburra (kōōk´ ə bûr´ ə)
kudos (kōō´ dōs)
knell (nel)
kiosk (kē´ osk´)
kibitzer (kib´ it sər)
kindhearted (kind´ härt´ id)
kleptomania (klep´ tō mā´ nē ə)

Directions: Write the above vocabulary words in alphabetical order below.

1. Kale
2. Kaolin
3. Keel
4. Keen
5. Kelp
6. Khaki
7. Kibitzer
8. Kilohertz
9. Kilowatt
10. Kindhearted
11. Kinesthetic
12. Kiosk
13. Kleptomania
14. Knave
15. Knell
16. Knoll
17. Kookaburra
18. Krill
19. Kudos
20. Kumquat

© Mark Twain Media, Inc., Publishers   41

Unit 11: "K" Words: *Skills and Practice*

Directions: Write a **synonym** from the list of vocabulary words below on the line. A **synonym** is a word that means the same or nearly the same.

kindhearted	knave	keen	knoll	kudos
kibitzer	khaki	kelp		

1. seaweed _kelp_
2. rascal _Knave_
3. tan _Khaki_
4. sharp _Keen_
5. meddler _Kibitzer_
6. mound _Knoll_
7. praise _Kudos_
8. sympathetic _Kindhearted_

> **Did You Know?** *Kilo* means "one thousand." The prefix *kilo-* is from French *kilo*, which came from Greek *chilioi*.

Directions: Match the noun with the correct vocabulary word.

kumquat	kale	kookaburra	krill	kaolin	knell

1. bird _Kookaburra_
2. fruit _Kumquat_
3. shellfish _Krill_
4. bell _Knell_
5. clay _Kaolin_
6. cabbage _Kale_

Directions: Write a sentence for each of the vocabulary words below on your own paper. Remember to check your spelling and punctuation.

kleptomania	kilohertz	keel	kilowatt	kiosk
kinesthetic				

Extend Your Vocabulary

1. Design a food chain using krill as one of the links.
2. Make a list of animals unique to Australia, such as the kookaburra.
3. Create a word map of the different shades of brown, including khaki.
4. Research the different learning styles, including kinesthetic learning. Write a report.

Unit 11: "K" Words: *Vocabulary Quiz*

Directions: Match each vocabulary word with the correct meaning. Write the word on the line next to the meaning.

kilohertz	keel	khaki	knoll	kinesthetic
kilowatt	kelp	knave	kudos	kookaburra
kumquat	krill	knell	kiosk	kleptomania
kibitzer	keen	kaolin	kale	kindhearted

1. _Kiosk_ small building with one or more sides open, used as a newsstand, a bandstand, or an opening to a subway
2. _Khaki_ dull, yellowish-brown color
3. _Kibitzer_ person who gives unwanted advice
4. _Kilowatt_ unit of electrical power equal to 1,000 watts
5. _Kaolin_ fine, white clay used in making porcelain
6. _Kookaburra_ a large kingfisher of Australia with a harsh, crackling voice
7. _Kleptomania_ abnormal, irresistible desire to steal, especially things that one does not need
8. _Keel_ main timber or steel piece that extends the whole length of the bottom of a ship or boat
9. _Keen_ sharp, cutting
10. _Knell_ sound of a bell rung slowly after a death or at a funeral
11. _Kale_ kind of cabbage that has loose, curled leaves that are eaten as a vegetable
12. _Knoll_ small, round hill
13. _Kinesthetic_ having to do with sensations of motion from the muscles and joints
14. _Kilohertz_ 1,000 hertz, used to express the frequency of radio waves
15. _Kindhearted_ having or showing a kind heart; kindly
16. _Kumquat_ yellow or orange fruit somewhat like a small orange
17. _Kelp_ large, tough, brown seaweed
18. _Kudos_ glory; fame
19. _Knave_ tricky, dishonest person; rogue
20. _krill_ small, shrimp-like shellfish that is eaten by whales and other sea animals

Unit 12: "L" Words: *Vocabulary List and Alphabetizing*

lacquer (lak´ ər)
laden (lād´ ən)
lavatory (lav´ ə tôr ē)
lunatic (lōō´ nə tik)
laborious (lə bôr´ ē əs)
listless (list´ lis)
lenient (lēn´ yənt)
larceny (lär´ sə nē)
loathe (lōth)
lank (langk)

lope (lōp)
lance (lans)
lichen (lī´ kən)
liberate (lib´ ə rāt)
lucid (lōō´ sid)
lurk (lûrk)
lynch (linch)
lax (laks)
lacerate (las´ ə rāt)
languish (lang´ gwish)

Directions: Write the above vocabulary words in alphabetical order below.

1. _laborious_
2. _lacerate_
3. _lacquer_
4. _laden_
5. _lance_
6. _languish_
7. _lanky_
8. _larceny_
9. _lavatory_
10. _lax_
11. _lenient_
12. _liberate_
13. _lichen_
14. _listless_
15. _loathe_
16. _lope_
17. _lucid_
18. _lunatic_
19. _lurk_
20. _lynch_

Unit 12: "L" Words: *Skills and Practice*

Directions: Write a **synonym** from the list of vocabulary words below on the line. A **synonym** is a word that means the same or nearly the same.

lacquer	lacerate	laden	lance	lunatic
lavatory	larceny	lurk		

1. burdened _laden_
2. idiotic _lunatic_
3. spear _lance_
4. sneak _lurk_
5. theft _larceny_
6. varnish _lacquer_
7. bathroom _lavatory_
8. mangle _lacerate_

> **Did You Know?** *Larceny* came into the English language about 600 years ago from French *larcin* and can be traced back to Latin, meaning "a bandit or hired soldier."

Directions: Write an **antonym** from the list of vocabulary words below on the line. An **antonym** is a word that means the opposite or nearly opposite.

lenient	lucid	lanky	laborious	liberate
listless	loathe	lax		

1. dull _lucid_
2. capture _liberate_
3. active _listless_
4. harsh _lenient_
5. lazy _laborious_
6. tight _lax_
7. love _loathe_
8. broad _lanky_

Directions: Write a sentence for each of the vocabulary words below on your own paper. Remember to check your spelling and punctuation.

lichen	lope	lynch	languish

Extend Your Vocabulary

1. Make a list of various words that mean "run," such as *lope*.
2. Write about something you "loathe." Give numerous reasons why.
3. Pretend you are a prisoner of war. Name the war, describe the conditions, and tell how you felt about being "liberated."
4. Research the plant "lichen." In what biome would you find it? Write a report.

Unit 12: "L" Words: *Vocabulary Quiz*

Name: _____ Date: _____

Directions: Match each vocabulary word with the correct meaning. Write the word on the line next to the meaning.

lacquer	lope	laden	lance	lavatory
lichen	lurk	lanky	lucid	liberate
larceny	lax	lynch	laborious	lunatic
listless	loathe	lenient	lacerate	languish

1. **lenient** mild or gentle; not harsh or stern
2. **lope** to run with a long, easy stride
3. **lurk** to stay hidden, ready to spring out or attack; to exist undiscovered or unobserved
4. **lavatory** bowl or basin to wash in; toilet
5. **loathe** feel strong dislike and disgust; intense aversion
6. **liberate** set free
7. **lynch** put an accused person to death, usually by hanging, without a lawful trial
8. **lacquer** varnish used to give a protective coating or a shiny appearance to metal or wood
9. **lacerate** tear roughly
10. **lucid** clear, transparent
11. **larceny** unlawful taking and using of the personal property of another person
12. **lance** long, wooden spear with a sharp iron or steel head
13. **lanky** long and thin; slender
14. **lunatic** insane; extremely foolish
15. **languish** grow weak; become weary; lose energy
16. **lichen** flowerless plant that looks somewhat like moss and consists of a fungus and an algae growing together as one plant
17. **lax** not firm or tight; slack
18. **laden** loaded
19. **laborious** requiring hard work; industrious
20. **listless** seeming too tired to care about anything; not interested in things; not caring to be active

© Mark Twain Media, Inc., Publishers   48

Unit 13: "M" Words: *Vocabulary List and Alphabetizing*

Name: _____ Date: _____

mishap (mis´ hap)	meddle (med´ əl)
midst (midst)	monotonous (mə not´ 'n əs)
mutiny (myōōt´ 'n ē)	maestro (mī´ strō)
morose (mə rōs´)	menace (men´ is)
menagerie (mə naj´ ər ē)	misguide (mis gīd´)
misfortune (mis fôr´ chən)	misnomer (mis nō´ mər)
matron (mā´ trən)	molten (mōlt´ 'n)
magistrate (maj´ is strāt)	mastication (mas´ ti kā´ shən)
misdemeanor (mis´ də mē´ nər)	misanthrope (mis´ ən thrōp)
meander (mē an´ dər)	memorandum (mem´ ə ran´ dəm)

Directions: Write the above vocabulary words in alphabetical order below.

1. maestro
2. magistrate
3. mastication
4. matron
5. meander
6. meddle
7. memorandum
8. menace
9. menagerie
10. midst
11. misanthrope
12. misdemeanor
13. misfortune
14. misguide
15. mishap
16. misnomer
17. molten
18. monotonous
19. morose
20. mutiny

© Mark Twain Media, Inc., Publishers   49

Unit 13: "M" Words: *Skills and Practice*

Name: _____ Date: _____

Directions: Write a **synonym** from the list of vocabulary words below on the line. A **synonym** is a word that means the same or nearly the same.

molten	mishap	magistrate	misguide	misfortune
meander	meddle	mastication	midst	memorandum

1. trouble — mishap
2. mislead — misguide
3. note — memorandum
4. interfere — meddle
5. leader — magistrate
6. calamity — misfortune
7. middle — midst
8. stroll — meander
9. chewing — mastication
10. melted — molten

Did You Know? The prefix *mis-* means "bad" or "wrong," as in *mispronunciation*.

Directions: Write an **antonym** from the list of vocabulary words below on the line. An **antonym** is a word that means the opposite or nearly opposite.

misanthrope	menace	mutiny	morose	monotonous

1. change — monotonous
2. cheerful — morose
3. obedience — mutiny
4. optimist — misanthrope
5. console — menace

Directions: Write a sentence for each of the vocabulary words below on your own paper. Remember to check your spelling and punctuation.

maestro	menagerie	misnomer	matron	misdemeanor

Extend Your Vocabulary

1. Write a narrative piece about a mishap that you experienced or saw happen. Remember to include your reactions and feelings.
2. Make a list of things that can be monotonous. Share and compare with a friend.
3. Research a great maestro and write a report. Include all parts of his or her life and what may have inspired him or her to pursue his or her musical career.
4. Create a list of misdemeanors and the consequences of committing a misdemeanor.

© Mark Twain Media, Inc., Publishers   51

Unit 13: "M" Words: *Vocabulary Quiz*

Name: _____ Date: _____

Directions: Match each vocabulary word with the correct meaning. Write the word on the line next to the meaning.

misnomer	meddle	midst	monotonous	memorandum
maestro	menace	matron	menagerie	misguide
misfortune	mishap	molten	magistrate	misanthrope
mastication	morose	mutiny	meander	misdemeanor

1. **matron** woman who manages the household matters of a school, hospital, or other institution
2. **midst** the middle part
3. **mastication** act of chewing
4. **maestro** great composer, teacher, or conductor of music
5. **misfortune** bad luck
6. **mishap** unlucky accident
7. **molten** made into liquid by heat
8. **mutiny** open rebellion against lawful authority, especially by sailors or soldiers against their officers
9. **misanthrope** person who dislikes or distrusts people in general
10. **menace** threaten; threat
11. **misnomer** name that describes wrongly
12. **meddle** busy oneself with or in other people's affairs without being asked or needed
13. **magistrate** government official who has power to apply the law and put it in force
14. **memorandum** short, written statement for future use
15. **meander** follow a winding course
16. **misguide** lead into mistakes or wrongdoing
17. **morose** gloomy; ill-humored; sullen
18. **monotonous** continuing in the same tone; without change
19. **menagerie** collection of wild animals kept in cages for exhibition
20. **misdemeanor** breaking of the law, not as serious as a felony

© Mark Twain Media, Inc., Publishers   52

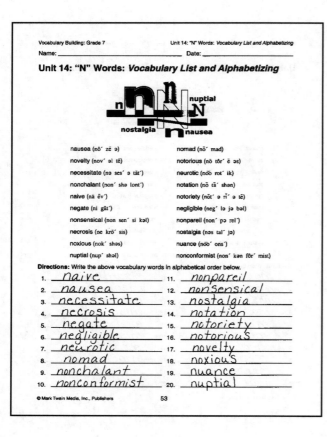

Name: _____   Date: _____

Unit 14: "N" Words: *Vocabulary List and Alphabetizing*

nausea (nô´ zē ə)   nomad (nō´ mad)
novelty (nov´ əl tē)   notorious (nō tôr´ ē əs)
necessitate (nə ses´ ə tāt´)   neurotic (nŏŏ rot´ ik)
nonchalant (non´ shə lont´)   notation (nō tā´ shən)
naive (nä ēv´)   notoriety (nōt´ ə rī´ ə tē)
negate (ni gāt´)   negligible (neg´ lə jə bəl)
nonsensical (non sen´ si kəl)   nonpareil (non´ pə rel´)
necrosis (ne krō´ sis)   nostalgia (nəs tal´ jə)
noxious (nok´ shəs)   nuance (nŏŏ´ ons´)
nuptial (nup´ shəl)   nonconformist (non´ kən fôr´ mist)

Directions: Write the above vocabulary words in alphabetical order below.

1. naive
2. nausea
3. necessitate
4. necrosis
5. negate
6. negligible
7. neurotic
8. nomad
9. nonchalant
10. nonconformist
11. nonpareil
12. nonsensical
13. nostalgia
14. notation
15. notoriety
16. notorious
17. novelty
18. noxious
19. nuance
20. nuptial

© Mark Twain Media, Inc., Publishers   53

Name: _____   Date: _____

Unit 14: "N" Words: *Skills and Practice*

Directions: Write a **synonym** from the list of vocabulary words below on the line. A **synonym** is a word that means the same or nearly the same.

necrosis	novelty	negate	notation	notorious
necessitate	notoriety	nausea		

1. well known notorious
2. jotting notation
3. loathing nausea
4. nullify negate
5. ill fame notoriety
6. newness novelty
7. force necessitate
8. decay necrosis

Did You Know? There are many prefixes that express negation in the English language. Some prefixes that mean "not" include *a-* as in *apathy*, *an-* as in *anorexia*, *ir-* as in *irregular*, *neg-* as in *negative*, and *non-* as in *nondescript*.

Directions: Write an **antonym** from the list of vocabulary words below on the line. An **antonym** is a word that means the opposite or nearly opposite.

negligible	nomad	noxious	nonsensical	nonconformist
nonchalant	naive			

1. settler nomad
2. conformer nonconformist
3. nonpoisonous noxious
4. concerned nonchalant
5. worldly-wise naive
6. wise nonsensical
7. noticeable negligible

Directions: Write a sentence for each of the vocabulary words below on your own paper. Remember to check your spelling and punctuation.

necessitate	nonpareil	nostalgia	nuance	nuptial

Extend Your Vocabulary

1. Research the nomadic tribes of Africa. Write a report about their lifestyles.
2. Compare and contrast the nuptial ceremonies of two different countries. Use a T-chart or Venn diagram.
3. List several people who are notorious and the reasons for their bad reputations.
4. List as many novelties as you can that are "in" right now. One example would be yo-yo's.

© Mark Twain Media, Inc., Publishers   55

Name: _____   Date: _____

Unit 14: "N" Words: *Vocabulary Quiz*

Directions: Match each vocabulary word with the correct meaning. Write the word on the line next to the meaning.

nausea	nomad	novelty	nuance	necessitate
neurotic	naive	nonchalant	notation	necrosis
notoriety	negate	negligible	nonpareil	nonsensical
nostalgia	noxious	notorious	nuptial	nonconformist

1. nonpareil person or thing having no equal
2. notorious well known or commonly known, especially because of something bad
3. negligible able to be disregarded
4. neurotic having or suffering from a neurosis or emotional disorder
5. nuance slight variation in expression, tone, feeling, or color
6. naive simple in nature, like a child; not sophisticated
7. nonsensical foolish or absurd
8. nausea the feeling that one has when about to vomit; extreme disgust
9. nonconformist one who refuses to conform or accept the established laws, rules, or customs of a group
10. nomad wanderer
11. necrosis the death or decay of tissue in a particular part of the body
12. necessitate make necessary; compel
13. noxious very harmful; poisonous
14. nonchalant without enthusiasm; indifferent
15. nostalgia painful yearning for one's home, country, city, or for anything far removed in space or time
16. notation note to assist memory; record
17. nuptial of marriage or weddings
18. negate destroy; make ineffective; deny
19. novelty novel character; a new or unusual thing
20. notoriety being famous for something bad; ill fame

© Mark Twain Media, Inc., Publishers   56

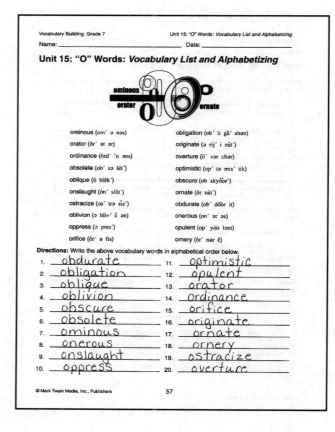

Name: _____   Date: _____

Unit 15: "O" Words: *Vocabulary List and Alphabetizing*

ominous (om´ ə nəs)   obligation (ob´ li gā´ shən)
orator (ôr´ ət ər)   originate (ə rij´ i nāt´)
ordinance (ôrd´ ´n əns)   overture (ō´ vər chər)
obsolete (ob´ sə lēt´)   optimistic (op´ tə mis´ tik)
oblique (ō blēk´)   obscure (ob skyōōr´)
onslaught (ôn´ slôt´)   ornate (ôr nāt´)
ostracize (os´ trə sīz´)   obdurate (ob´ dŏŏr it)
oblivion (ə bliv´ ē ən)   onerous (on´ ər əs)
oppress (ə pres´)   opulent (op´ yŏŏ lənt)
orifice (ôr´ ə fis)   ornery (ôr´ nər ē)

Directions: Write the above vocabulary words in alphabetical order below.

1. obdurate
2. obligation
3. oblique
4. oblivion
5. obscure
6. obsolete
7. ominous
8. onerous
9. onslaught
10. oppress
11. optimistic
12. opulent
13. orator
14. ordinance
15. orifice
16. originate
17. ornate
18. ornery
19. ostracize
20. overture

© Mark Twain Media, Inc., Publishers   57

Unit 15 "O" Words: *Skills and Practice*

Directions: Write a **synonym** from the list of vocabulary words below on the line. A **synonym** is a word that means the same or nearly the same.

onslaught	obligation	overture	orator	oblique
obsolete	onerous	obdurate		

1. burdensome **onerous**
2. indirect **oblique**
3. offer **overture**
4. speaker **orator**
5. old-fashioned **obsolete**
6. assault **onslaught**
7. duty **obligation**
8. obstinate **obdurate**

Did You Know? *Overture* came into the English language about 600 years ago from French *overture*, which came from Latin, meaning "opening."

Directions: Write an **antonym** from the list of vocabulary words below on the line. An **antonym** is a word that means the opposite or nearly opposite.

opulent	ornate	ominous	ostracize	optimistic
obscure	ornery	originate	obdurate	

1. flexible **obdurate**
2. pessimistic **optimistic**
3. favorable **ominous**
4. kind **ornery**
5. clear **obscure**
6. accept **ostracize**
7. end **originate**
8. poor **opulent**
9. plain **ornate**

Directions: Write a sentence for each of the vocabulary words below on your own paper. Remember to check your spelling and punctuation.

oblivion	ordinance	oppress	orifice

Extend Your Vocabulary

1. List as many words as you can that have multiple meanings such as *overture*.
2. Research your last name. Where did it originate? What does it mean? Write a mini-report.
3. Write a report on one great orator. (Greek, Roman, etc.)
4. Write about an obligation you have with your family. How does it make you feel?

© Mark Twain Media, Inc., Publishers   59

Unit 15 "O" Words: *Vocabulary Quiz*

Directions: Match each vocabulary word with the correct meaning. Write the word on the line next to the meaning.

ominous	obligation	orator	originate	ordinance
overture	obsolete	optimistic	oblique	obscure
onslaught	ostracize	obdurate	oblivion	onerous
oppress	opulent	orifice	ornery	ornate

1. **oblivion** condition of being entirely forgotten
2. **ominous** unfavorable; threatening
3. **ostracize** shut out from society, favor, or privileges
4. **originate** invent; begin; arise
5. **oppress** govern harshly; keep down unjustly or by cruelty
6. **optimistic** looks on the bright side of things
7. **orifice** opening or hole; mouth
8. **obscure** not clearly expressed; hard to understand; vague
9. **ornery** mean in disposition
10. **ordinance** established rule, rite, or law
11. **obdurate** stubborn or unyielding
12. **obligation** binding power of a law, promise, or sense of duty
13. **onerous** hard to carry or take
14. **orator** person who speaks very well in public
15. **opulent** having wealth; rich
16. **obsolete** no longer in use; out of date
17. **oblique** not straightforward
18. **onslaught** vigorous attack
19. **overture** proposal or offer; musical composition played at the beginning of an opera or symphony
20. **ornate** much adorned; much ornamented

© Mark Twain Media, Inc., Publishers   60

Unit 16: "P" Words: *Vocabulary List and Alphabetizing*

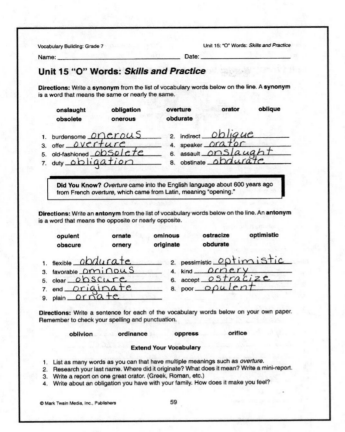

predicament (prē dik´ ə mənt)
propaganda (prop´ ə gan´ də)
predominant (prē dom´ ə nənt)
provision (prə vizh´ ən)
premonition (prem´ ə nish´ ən)
pugnacious (pug nā´ shəs)
postulate (pos´ chə lāt´)
pretentious (prē ten´ shəs)
peripatetic (per´ i pə tet´ ik)
privy (priv´ ē)

preside (prē zīd´)
prosperous (pros´ pər əs)
propulsion (prə pul´ shən)
prelude (prā´ lōōd)
preposterous (prē pos´ tər əs)
periodical (pir´ ē od´ i kəl)
predatory (pred´ ə tôr´ ē)
profound (prō found´)
posthumous (pos´ chōō məs)
punctilious (pungk til´ ē əs)

Directions: Write the above vocabulary words in alphabetical order below.

1. **periodical**
2. **peripatetic**
3. **posthumous**
4. **postulate**
5. **predatory**
6. **predicament**
7. **predominant**
8. **prelude**
9. **premonition**
10. **preposterous**
11. **preside**
12. **pretentious**
13. **privy**
14. **profound**
15. **propaganda**
16. **propulsion**
17. **prosperous**
18. **provision**
19. **pugnacious**
20. **punctilious**

© Mark Twain Media, Inc., Publishers   61

Unit 16: "P" Words: *Skills and Practice*

Directions: Write a **synonym** from the list of vocabulary words below on the line. A **synonym** is a word that means the same or nearly the same.

prosperous	predominant	prelude	profound	predicament
provision	periodical	postulate	premonition	

1. introduction **prelude**
2. thriving **prosperous**
3. claim **postulate**
4. prevailing **predominant**
5. great **profound**
6. preparation **provision**
7. magazine **periodical**
8. dilemma **predicament**
9. forewarning **premonition**

Did You Know? The prefix *pre-* means "before," as in *prewar*. The prefix *post-* means "after in time" or "later," as in *postscript*.

Directions: Write an **antonym** from the list of vocabulary words below on the line. An **antonym** is a word that means the opposite or nearly opposite.

predatory	punctilious	privy	preposterous	pretentious
peripatetic	pugnacious			

1. logical **preposterous**
2. prey **predatory**
3. public **privy**
4. humble **pretentious**
5. peaceable **pugnacious**
6. inaccurate **punctilious**
7. homebody **peripatetic**

Directions: Write a sentence for each of the vocabulary words below on your own paper. Remember to check your spelling and punctuation.

preside	propaganda	propulsion	posthumous

Extend Your Vocabulary

1. Watch a sample of television commercials. Notice the propaganda techniques used. Give examples.
2. Tell a preposterous story to a friend.
3. Make a list of periodicals.
4. Write a persuasive piece about why you think someone is prosperous, but not necessarily wealthy.

© Mark Twain Media, Inc., Publishers   63

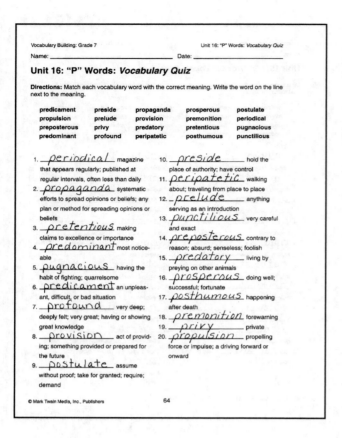

Unit 16: "P" Words: *Vocabulary Quiz*

Directions: Match each vocabulary word with the correct meaning. Write the word on the line next to the meaning.

predicament	preside	propaganda	prosperous	postulate
propulsion	prelude	provision	premonition	periodical
preposterous	privy	predatory	pretentious	pugnacious
predominant	profound	peripatetic	posthumous	punctilious

1. _periodical_ magazine that appears regularly; published at regular intervals, often less than daily
2. _propaganda_ systematic efforts to spread opinions or beliefs; any plan or method for spreading opinions or beliefs
3. _pretentious_ making claims to excellence or importance
4. _predominant_ most noticeable
5. _pugnacious_ having the habit of fighting; quarrelsome
6. _predicament_ an unpleasant, difficult, or bad situation
7. _profound_ very deep; deeply felt; very great; having or showing great knowledge
8. _provision_ act of providing; something provided or prepared for the future
9. _postulate_ assume without proof; take for granted; require; demand
10. _preside_ hold the place of authority; have control
11. _peripatetic_ walking about; traveling from place to place
12. _prelude_ anything serving as an introduction
13. _punctilious_ very careful and exact
14. _preposterous_ contrary to reason; absurd; senseless; foolish
15. _predatory_ living by preying on other animals
16. _prosperous_ doing well; successful; fortunate
17. _posthumous_ happening after death
18. _premonition_ forewarning
19. _privy_ private
20. _propulsion_ propelling force or impulse; a driving forward or onward

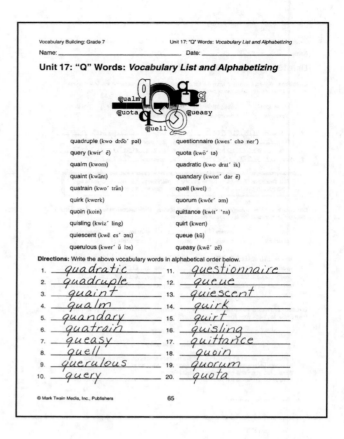

Unit 17: "Q" Words: *Vocabulary List and Alphabetizing*

quadruple (kwo drŏŏ′ pəl)	questionnaire (kwes′ chə ner′)
query (kwir′ ē)	quota (kwō′ tə)
qualm (kwom)	quadratic (kwo drat′ ik)
quaint (kwānt)	quandary (kwon′ dər ē)
quatrain (kwo′ trān)	quell (kwel)
quirk (kwerk)	quorum (kwôr′ əm)
quoin (koin)	quittance (kwit′ 'ns)
quisling (kwiz′ ling)	quirt (kwert)
quiescent (kwē es′ ənt)	queue (kū)
querulous (kwer′ ū los)	queasy (kwē′ zē)

Directions: Write the above vocabulary words in alphabetical order below.

1. _quadratic_
2. _quadruple_
3. _quaint_
4. _qualm_
5. _quandary_
6. _quatrain_
7. _queasy_
8. _quell_
9. _querulous_
10. _query_
11. _questionnaire_
12. _queue_
13. _quiescent_
14. _quirk_
15. _quirt_
16. _quisling_
17. _quittance_
18. _quoin_
19. _quorum_
20. _quota_

Unit 17: "Q" Words: *Skills and Practice*

Directions: Write a **synonym** from the list of vocabulary words below on the line. A **synonym** is a word that means the same or nearly the same.

quaint	quirt	quadruple	quoin	queue
queasy	quirk	quittance	qualm	quota

1. line _queue_
2. mannerism _quirk_
3. portion _quota_
4. cornerstone _quoin_
5. fourfold _quadruple_
6. receipt _quittance_
7. whip _quirt_
8. doubt _qualm_
9. unusual _quaint_
10. squeamish _queasy_

> **Did You Know?** *Questionnaire* has the base word *question*. *Question* came into the English language about 700 years ago from the French *questiun*. It can be traced back to the Latin word, *quaerere*, meaning "to seek, ask."

Directions: Write an **antonym** from the list of vocabulary words below on the line. An **antonym** is a word that means the opposite or nearly opposite.

quandary	quell	query	quisling	querulous
quiescent				

1. answer _query_
2. loyalist _quisling_
3. certainty _quandary_
4. encourage _quell_
5. boisterous _quiescent_
6. easygoing _querulous_

Directions: Write a sentence for each of the vocabulary words below on your own paper. Remember to check your spelling and punctuation.

questionnaire	quadratic	quatrain	quorum

Extend Your Vocabulary

1. Create a questionnaire about a subject that interests you. Survey 50 people, and make a graph of the results.
2. Write a narrative piece about someone who is facing a quandary.
3. Describe a quaint place you would like to visit. Use the Internet to help you.
4. List as many quislings in American history as you can. Why were they quislings?

Unit 17: "Q" Words: *Vocabulary Quiz*

Directions: Match each vocabulary word with the correct meaning. Write the word on the line next to the meaning.

quadruple	questionnaire	quisling	qualm	quadratic
quittance	quandary	quaint	quell	quiescent
quatrain	quorum	quirk	query	querulous
quoin	quirt	queasy	quota	queue

1. _quittance_ release from debt or obligation; the paper certifying this
2. _questionnaire_ written or printed list of questions used to gather information or to obtain a sampling of opinions
3. _quirk_ peculiar way of acting
4. _quota_ share of the total due from or to a particular district, state, or person
5. _quirt_ riding whip with a short, stout handle and a lash of braided leather
6. _quaint_ strange or odd in an interesting, pleasing, or amusing way
7. _queasy_ inclined to nausea; easily upset
8. _quell_ put down; overcome; subdue
9. _quorum_ minimum number of members of any society or assembly needed to transact business in a legal or binding way
10. _quadruple_ consisting of four parts; including four parts or parties; four times
11. _quoin_ outside angle or corner of a wall or building
12. _query_ question; inquiry
13. _quisling_ person who treacherously helps prepare the way for enemy occupation of his own country
14. _qualm_ sudden disturbing feeling in the mind; uneasiness
15. _queue_ a line, for example of people or automobiles
16. _quandary_ state of perplexity or uncertainty
17. _quiescent_ inactive; quiet; still
18. _quatrain_ stanza or poem of four lines
19. _quadratic_ of or like a square
20. _querulous_ complaining; fretful; peevish

Top Left Worksheet

Unit 18: "R" Words: *Vocabulary List and Alphabetizing*

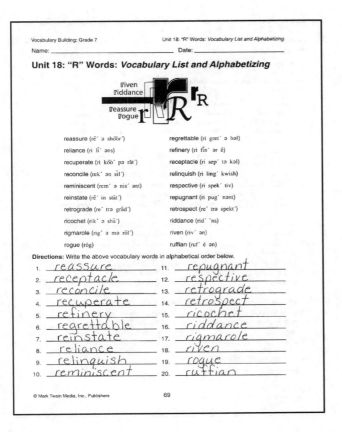

reassure (rē´ ə shŏŏr´)
reliance (ri lī´ əns)
recuperate (ri kōō´ pə rāt´)
reconcile (rek´ ən sīl´)
reminiscent (rem´ ə nis´ ənt)
reinstate (rē´ in stāt´)
retrograde (re´ trə grād´)
ricochet (rik´ ə shā´)
rigmarole (rig´ ə mə rōl´)
rogue (rōg)

regrettable (ri gret´ ə bəl)
refinery (ri fīn´ ər ē)
receptacle (ri sep´ tə kəl)
relinquish (ri ling´ kwish)
respective (ri spek´ tiv)
repugnant (ri pug´ nənt)
retrospect (re´ trə spekt´)
riddance (rid´ ´ns)
riven (riv´ ən)
ruffian (ruf´ ē ən)

Directions: Write the above vocabulary words in alphabetical order below.

1. reassure
2. receptacle
3. reconcile
4. recuperate
5. refinery
6. regrettable
7. reinstate
8. reliance
9. relinquish
10. reminiscent
11. repugnant
12. respective
13. retrograde
14. retrospect
15. ricochet
16. riddance
17. rigmarole
18. riven
19. rogue
20. ruffian

  69

Top Right Worksheet

Unit 18: "R" Words: *Skills and Practice*

Directions: Write a **synonym** from the list of vocabulary words below on the line. A **synonym** is a word that means the same or nearly the same.

regrettable	reconcile	ruffian	riddance	respective
rigmarole	reassure	rogue	ricochet	receptacle
reminiscent	repugnant			

1. sorrowful — regrettable
2. reunite — reconcile
3. removal — riddance
4. guarantee — reassure
5. container — receptacle
6. distasteful — repugnant
7. recall — reminiscent
8. individual — respective
9. rebound — ricochet
10. nonsense — rigmarole
11. rascal — rogue
12. bully — ruffian

> **Did You Know?** The prefix *re-* can mean "back" in such words as *recall, reflect,* or *repay.* It can also mean "again" in such words as *reappear, recopy,* or *redo.*

Directions: Write an **antonym** from the list of vocabulary words below on the line. An **antonym** is a word that means the opposite or nearly opposite.

| riven | retrograde | recuperate | relinquish | reliance |

1. resist — relinquish
2. repaired — riven
3. mistrust — reliance
4. onward — retrograde
5. regress — recuperate

Directions: Write a sentence for each of the vocabulary words below on your own paper. Remember to check your spelling and punctuation.

| refinery | reinstate | retrospect |

Extend Your Vocabulary

1. If there were a ruffian in your class, what could you do? Why? Write about it.
2. List some repugnant smells or odors. Why are some odors repugnant to you and others aren't?
3. Research and write about oil refineries. Include their locations, values, problems, and impact on the environment.
4. Describe a situation that was regrettable to you. What could you have done differently?

  71

Bottom Left Worksheet

Unit 18: "R" Words: *Vocabulary Quiz*

Directions: Match each vocabulary word with the correct meaning. Write the word on the line next to the meaning.

reassure	regrettable	reliance	recuperate	ruffian
receptacle	reconcile	relinquish	reminiscent	riven
respective	reinstate	repugnant	retrograde	rogue
retrospect	ricochet	riddance	rigmarole	refinery

1. repugnant — disagreeable or offensive
2. reassurance — restore to confidence
3. reinstate — put back in a former position or condition; establish again
4. refinery — building and machinery for purifying petroleum, sugar, or other things
5. riddance — clearing away or out
6. reconcile — make friends again; settle a difference or quarrel
7. retrograde — moving backward; retreating
8. regrettable — deserving or giving cause for regret
9. rigmarole — foolish talk or activity; words or action without meaning
10. relinquish — give up; let go
11. rogue — dishonest or unprincipled person; mischievous person
12. respective — belong to each; particular
13. retrospect — survey of past time or events; thinking about the past
14. recuperate — recover from sickness, exhaustion, or loss
15. riven — torn apart, split
16. receptacle — any container or place used to keep items contained conveniently
17. ruffian — brutal, rough, or cruel person; hoodlum
18. reminiscent — recalling past persons or events
19. ricochet — move with a jumping or skipping motion
20. reliance — trust or dependence

  72

Bottom Right Worksheet

Unit 19: "S" Words: *Vocabulary List and Alphabetizing*

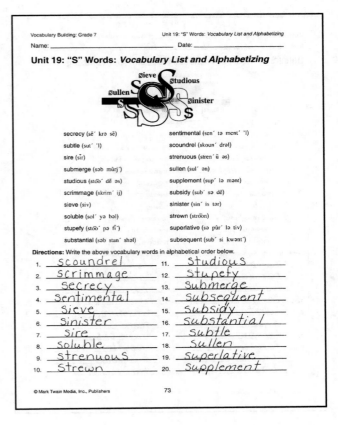

secrecy (sē´ krə sē)
subtle (sut´ ´l)
sire (sīr)
submerge (səb mûrj´)
studious (stōō´ dē əs)
scrimmage (skrim´ ij)
sieve (siv)
soluble (sol´ yə bəl)
stupefy (stōō´ pə fī´)
substantial (səb stan´ shəl)

sentimental (sen´ tə mənt ´l)
scoundrel (skoun´ drəl)
strenuous (stren´ ū əs)
sullen (sul´ ən)
supplement (sup´ lə mənt)
subsidy (sub´ sə dē)
sinister (sin´ is tər)
strewn (strōōn)
superlative (sə pûr´ lə tiv)
subsequent (sub´ si kwənt´)

Directions: Write the above vocabulary words in alphabetical order below.

1. scoundrel
2. scrimmage
3. secrecy
4. sentimental
5. sieve
6. sinister
7. sire
8. soluble
9. strenuous
10. strewn
11. studious
12. stupefy
13. submerge
14. subsequent
15. subsidy
16. substantial
17. subtle
18. sullen
19. superlative
20. supplement

  73

Unit 19: "S" Words: Skills and Practice

Directions: Write a **synonym** from the list of vocabulary words below on the line. A synonym is a word that means the same or nearly the same.

| sieve | scoundrel | strewn | scrimmage | supplement |
| sire | stupefy | studious | subsidy | superlative |

1. supreme _Superlative_
2. forefather _sire_
3. thoughtful _studious_
4. rogue _scoundrel_
5. grant _subsidy_
6. senseless _stupefy_
7. addition _supplement_
8. struggle _scrimmage_
9. strainer _sieve_
10. scattered _strewn_

Did You Know? The prefix *sub-* means "under or below." Many of our words, such as *subnormal*, begin with this prefix. It can also mean "lower or subordinate," as in *subcommittee.*

Directions: Write an **antonym** from the list of vocabulary words below on the line. An antonym is a word that means the opposite or nearly opposite.

| submerge | sentimental | subtle | substantial | sullen |
| strenuous | subsequent | sinister |

1. surface _submerge_
2. pleasant _sullen_
3. practical _sentimental_
4. virtuous _sinister_
5. overt _subtle_
6. preceding _subsequent_
7. unimportant _substantial_
8. easy _strenuous_

Directions: Write a sentence for each of the vocabulary words below on your own paper. Remember to check your spelling and punctuation.

secrecy   soluble

Extend Your Vocabulary

1. Experiment with items that are soluble in water. Write about your discoveries.
2. List the skills that a studious student needs to be successful.
3. Write about a time when you were sentimental. Include when it happened, where you were, and what happened to cause you to feel that way.
4. Make a list of different words for scoundrel. Tell about a scoundrel in a book you have read. What made him a scoundrel? Was he successful, or did the "good guys" win?

Unit 19: "S" Words: Vocabulary Quiz

Directions: Match each vocabulary word with the correct meaning. Write the word on the line next to the meaning.

secrecy	sentimental	subtle	scoundrel	stupefy
strenuous	submerge	sullen	studious	sieve
supplement	scrimmage	subsidy	sinister	strewn
superlative	subsequent	soluble	substantial	sire

1. _sieve_ utensil with many tiny holes for separating the finer from the coarser parts of a substance.
2. _secrecy_ condition of being secret or of being kept secret
3. _strewn_ scattered or sprinkled
4. _strenuous_ very active; requiring much energy
5. _subsidy_ grant or contribution of money, especially one made by a government
6. _subtle_ not obvious; delicate; fine
7. _stupefy_ make stupid, dull; astound; overwhelm with shock
8. _studious_ fond of study; showing careful consideration; careful
9. _sinister_ threatening; bad; evil; dishonest
10. _scoundrel_ wicked person without honor or good principles
11. _Superlative_ of the highest kind; above all others
12. _supplement_ something added to complete something or to make it larger or better
13. _subsequent_ after; following; later
14. _scrimmage_ rough fight or struggle
15. _soluble_ capable of being dissolved
16. _sire_ male ancestor; male parent
17. _sullen_ silent because of bad humor or anger
18. _sentimental_ having or showing much tender feeling
19. _substantial_ material; real; large; important
20. _submerge_ put under water; cover with water

Unit 20: "T" Words: Vocabulary List and Alphabetizing

torrent
taut
toil
tabor

toil (toil)
transmit (trans mit´)
turmoil (tər´ moil´)
tether (teth´ ər)
trestle (tres´ əl)
tithe (tith)
taut (tôt)
tandem (tan´ dəm)
tantalize (tan´ tə līz´)
tempest (tem´ pist)

torrent (tôr´ ənt)
transfusion (trans fū´ zhən)
tangible (tan´ jə bəl)
transpose (trans pōz´)
tumult (tōō´ mult)
transcend (tran send´)
tabor (tā´ bər)
tankard (tang´ kərd)
transparent (trans per´ ənt)
tenacious (tə nā´ shəs)

Directions: Write the above vocabulary words in alphabetical order below.

1. _tabor_
2. _tandem_
3. _tangible_
4. _tankard_
5. _tantalize_
6. _taut_
7. _tempest_
8. _tenacious_
9. _tether_
10. _tithe_
11. _toil_
12. _torrent_
13. _transcend_
14. _transfusion_
15. _transmit_
16. _transparent_
17. _transpose_
18. _trestle_
19. _tumult_
20. _turmoil_

Unit 20: "T" Words: Skills and Practice

Directions: Write a **synonym** from the list of vocabulary words below on the line. A synonym is a word that means the same or nearly the same.

| torrent | tantalize | tankard | transcend | toil |
| transpose | tempest | tumult | tabor |

1. exceed _transcend_
2. mug _tankard_
3. flood _torrent_
4. drum _tabor_
5. labor _toil_
6. tease _tantalize_
7. interchange _transpose_
8. commotion _tumult_
9. windstorm _tempest_

Did You Know? *Tantalize* came from the name of Tantalus, a king in a Greek myth. After his death, his spirit was punished by having to stand in water under branches of a tree filled with fruit. When Tantalus reached for some fruit, it receded from his grasp. When he bent down to drink, the water drained away.

Directions: Write an **antonym** from the list of vocabulary words below on the line. An antonym is a word that means the opposite or nearly opposite.

| turmoil | transmit | transparent | taut | tangible | tenacious |

1. opaque _transparent_
2. calmness _turmoil_
3. loose _taut_
4. retain _transmit_
5. abstract _tangible_
6. yielding _tenacious_

Directions: Write a sentence for each of the vocabulary words below on your own paper. Remember to check your spelling and punctuation.

transfusion   tether   tandem   trestle   tithe

Extend Your Vocabulary

1. Explain the meaning of the phrase "at the end of one's tether."
2. Research and write about the picture showing three soldiers marching during the American Revolution. One is carrying a flag, another a tabor, and the last a fife.
3. Write about the pros and cons of blood transfusions. Use a T-chart or Venn diagram to help organize your thoughts.
4. Write a narrative piece about a time you toiled for something. Include how you felt, what happened, and so on.

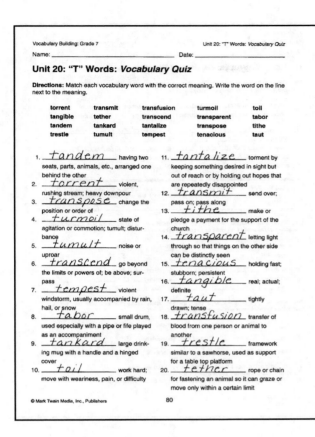

Unit 20: "T" Words: *Vocabulary Quiz*

Directions: Match each vocabulary word with the correct meaning. Write the word on the line next to the meaning.

torrent	transmit	transfusion	turmoil	toil
tangible	tether	transcend	transparent	tabor
tandem	tankard	tantalize	transpose	tithe
trestle	tumult	tempest	tenacious	taut

1. _tandem_ having two seats, parts, animals, etc., arranged one behind the other
2. _torrent_ violent, rushing stream; heavy downpour
3. _transpose_ change the position or order of
4. _turmoil_ state of agitation or commotion; tumult; disturbance
5. _tumult_ noise or uproar
6. _transcend_ go beyond the limits or powers of; be above; surpass
7. _tempest_ violent windstorm, usually accompanied by rain, hail, or snow
8. _tabor_ small drum, used especially with a pipe or fife played as an accompaniment
9. _tankard_ large drinking mug with a handle and a hinged cover
10. _toil_ work hard; move with weariness, pain, or difficulty
11. _tantalize_ torment by keeping something desired in sight but out of reach or by holding out hopes that are repeatedly disappointed
12. _transmit_ send over; pass on; pass along
13. _tithe_ make or pledge a payment for the support of the church
14. _transparent_ letting light through so that things on the other side can be distinctly seen
15. _tenacious_ holding fast; stubborn; persistent
16. _tangible_ real; actual; definite
17. _taut_ tightly drawn; tense
18. _transfusion_ transfer of blood from one person or animal to another
19. _trestle_ framework similar to a sawhorse, used as support for a table top platform
20. _tether_ rope or chain for fastening an animal so it can graze or move only within a certain limit

© Mark Twain Media, Inc., Publishers   80

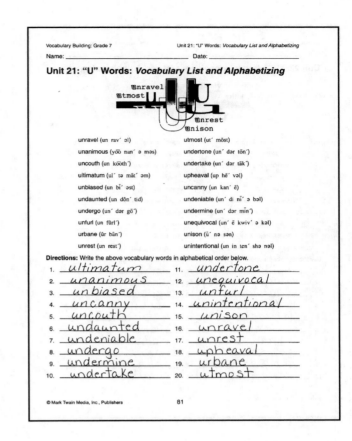

Unit 21: "U" Words: *Vocabulary List and Alphabetizing*

unravel (un rav´ əl) utmost (ut´ mōst)
unanimous (yōō nan´ ə məs) undertone (un´ dər tōn´)
uncouth (un kōōth´) undertake (un´ dər tāk´)
ultimatum (ul´ tə mā´ əm) upheaval (up hē´ vəl)
unbiased (un bī´ əst) uncanny (un kan´ ē)
undaunted (un dôn´ tid) undeniable (un´ di nī´ ə bəl)
undergo (un´ dər gō´) undermine (un´ dər mīn´)
unfurl (un fûrl´) unequivocal (un´ ē kwiv´ ə kəl)
urbane (ûr bān´) unison (ū´ nə sən)
unrest (un rest´) unintentional (un in ten´ shə nəl)

Directions: Write the above vocabulary words in alphabetical order below.

1. _ultimatum_
2. _unanimous_
3. _unbiased_
4. _uncanny_
5. _uncouth_
6. _undaunted_
7. _undeniable_
8. _undergo_
9. _undermine_
10. _undertake_
11. _undertone_
12. _unequivocal_
13. _unfurl_
14. _unintentional_
15. _unison_
16. _unravel_
17. _unrest_
18. _upheaval_
19. _urbane_
20. _utmost_

© Mark Twain Media, Inc., Publishers   81

Unit 21 "U" Words: *Skills and Practice*

Directions: Write a **synonym** from the list of vocabulary words below on the line. A **synonym** is a word that means the same or nearly the same.

unison	unequivocal	upheaval	undergo	urbane
unravel	undeniable	uncanny	unfurl	

1. turmoil _upheaval_
2. weird _uncanny_
3. suffer _undergo_
4. agreement _unison_
5. certain _undeniable_
6. separate _unravel_
7. unfold _unfurl_
8. plain _unequivocal_
9. elegant _urbane_

> **Did You Know?** The prefix *un-* means "not," and the prefix *under-* means "below."

Directions: Write an **antonym** from the list of vocabulary words below on the line. An **antonym** is a word that means the opposite or nearly opposite.

undertake	utmost	undaunted	unrest	uncouth
unanimous	unbiased	unintentional		

1. disagreed _unanimous_
2. avoid _undertake_
3. prejudiced _unbiased_
4. littlest _utmost_
5. refined _uncouth_
6. fearful _undaunted_
7. planned _unintentional_
8. ease _unrest_

Directions: Write a sentence for each of the vocabulary words below on your own paper. Remember to check your spelling and punctuation.

undertone	ultimatum	undermine

Extend Your Vocabulary

1. Make as many opposites as you can using the prefix *un-*. For example: biased/unbiased, bearable/unbearable.
2. List some hardships the pioneers had to undergo in America.
3. There have been times of unrest in America's history. Write about one of those times.
4. Write a persuasive piece about whether someone can be unbiased in politics.

© Mark Twain Media, Inc., Publishers   83

Unit 21: "U" Words: *Vocabulary Quiz*

Directions: Match each vocabulary word with the correct meaning. Write the word on the line next to the meaning.

unravel	utmost	unanimous	undertone	uncouth
undertake	ultimatum	upheaval	unbiased	uncanny
unison	undeniable	undergo	undermine	unfurl
unrest	unequivocal	unintentional	undaunted	urbane

1. _undaunted_ not afraid; not discouraged; fearless
2. _unanimous_ in complete accord or agreement; agreed
3. _undermine_ weaken by secret or unfair means
4. _undertake_ set about; try; attempt
5. _unison_ agreement; at the same time
6. _upheaval_ sudden or violent agitation; great turmoil
7. _undergo_ endure
8. _unravel_ separate the threads of; pull apart; come apart
9. _urbane_ courteous; refined
10. _unbiased_ impartial; fair
11. _unequivocal_ clear; plain
12. _undertone_ low or very quiet tone
13. _undeniable_ beyond denial or dispute
14. _utmost_ greatest possible; greatest; highest
15. _unintentional_ not intentional; not done purposely
16. _ultimatum_ final offer or demand given with the threat of severe penalties if refused
17. _unfurl_ spread out; shake out
18. _uncouth_ not refined; awkward; clumsy; crude
19. _uncanny_ strange and mysterious
20. _unrest_ lack of ease and quiet; restlessness

© Mark Twain Media, Inc., Publishers   84

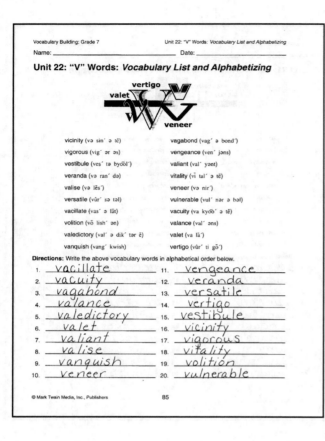

Vocabulary Building: Grade 7   Unit 22: "V" Words: *Vocabulary List and Alphabetizing*
Name: _____ Date: _____

Unit 22: "V" Words: *Vocabulary List and Alphabetizing*

vicinity (və sin´ ə tē)
vigorous (vig´ ər əs)
vestibule (ves´ tə byōōl)
veranda (və ran´ də)
valise (və lēs´)
versatile (vûr´ sə təl)
vacillate (vas´ ə lāt)
volition (võ lish´ ən)
valedictory (val´ ə dik´ tər ē)
vanquish (vang´ kwish)

vagabond (vag´ ə bond´)
vengeance (ven´ jəns)
valiant (val´ yənt)
vitality (vī tal´ ə tē)
veneer (və nir´)
vulnerable (vul´ nər ə bəl)
vacuity (və kyōō´ ə tē)
valance (val´ əns)
valet (va lā´)
vertigo (vûr´ ti gō´)

Directions: Write the above vocabulary words in alphabetical order below.

1. vacillate
2. vacuity
3. vagabond
4. valance
5. valedictory
6. valet
7. valiant
8. valise
9. vanquish
10. veneer
11. vengeance
12. veranda
13. versatile
14. vertigo
15. vestibule
16. vicinity
17. vigorous
18. vitality
19. volition
20. vulnerable

© Mark Twain Media, Inc., Publishers   85

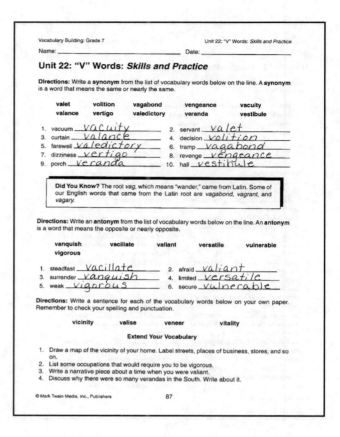

Vocabulary Building: Grade 7   Unit 22: "V" Words: *Skills and Practice*
Name: _____ Date: _____

Unit 22: "V" Words: *Skills and Practice*

Directions: Write a synonym from the list of vocabulary words below on the line. A synonym is a word that means the same or nearly the same.

valet   volition   vagabond   vengeance   vacuity
valance   vertigo   valedictory   veranda   vestibule

1. vacuum vacuity
2. servant valet
3. curtain valance
4. decision volition
5. farewell valedictory
6. tramp vagabond
7. dizziness vertigo
8. revenge vengeance
9. porch veranda
10. hall vestibule

Did You Know? The root *vag*, which means "wander," came from Latin. Some of our English words that came from the Latin root are *vagabond*, *vagrant*, and *vagary*.

Directions: Write an antonym from the list of vocabulary words below on the line. An antonym is a word that means the opposite or nearly opposite.

vanquish   vacillate   valiant   versatile   vulnerable
vigorous

1. steadfast vacillate
2. afraid valiant
3. surrender vanquish
4. limited versatile
5. weak vigorous
6. secure vulnerable

Directions: Write a sentence for each of the vocabulary words below on your own paper. Remember to check your spelling and punctuation.

vicinity   valise   veneer   vitality

Extend Your Vocabulary

1. Draw a map of the vicinity of your home. Label streets, places of business, stores, and so on.
2. List some occupations that would require you to be vigorous.
3. Write a narrative piece about a time when you were valiant.
4. Discuss why there were so many verandas in the South. Write about it.

© Mark Twain Media, Inc., Publishers   87

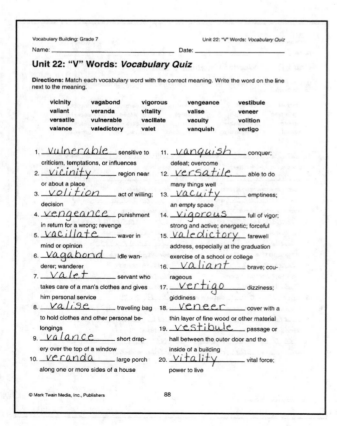

Vocabulary Building: Grade 7   Unit 22: "V" Words: *Vocabulary Quiz*
Name: _____ Date: _____

Unit 22: "V" Words: *Vocabulary Quiz*

Directions: Match each vocabulary word with the correct meaning. Write the word on the line next to the meaning.

vicinity   vagabond   vigorous   vengeance   vestibule
valiant   veranda   vitality   valise   veneer
versatile   vulnerable   vacillate   vacuity   volition
valance   valedictory   valet   vanquish   vertigo

1. vulnerable sensitive to criticism, temptations, or influences
2. vicinity region near or about a place
3. volition act of willing; decision
4. vengeance punishment in return for a wrong; revenge
5. vacillate waver in mind or opinion
6. vagabond idle wanderer; wanderer
7. valet servant who takes care of a man's clothes and gives him personal service
8. valise traveling bag to hold clothes and other personal belongings
9. valance short drapery over the top of a window
10. veranda large porch along one or more sides of a house
11. vanquish conquer; defeat; overcome
12. versatile able to do many things well
13. vacuity emptiness; an empty space
14. vigorous full of vigor; strong and active; energetic; forceful
15. valedictory farewell address, especially at the graduation exercise of a school or college
16. valiant brave; courageous
17. vertigo dizziness; giddiness
18. veneer cover with a thin layer of fine wood or other material
19. vestibule passage or hall between the outer door and the inside of a building
20. vitality vital force; power to live

© Mark Twain Media, Inc., Publishers   88

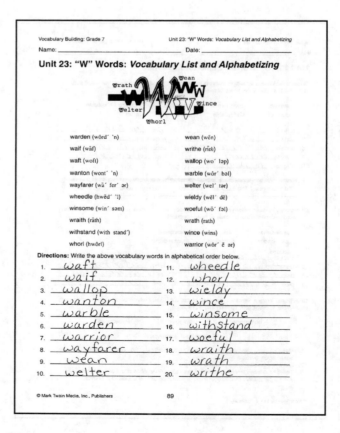

Vocabulary Building: Grade 7   Unit 23: "W" Words: *Vocabulary List and Alphabetizing*
Name: _____ Date: _____

Unit 23: "W" Words: *Vocabulary List and Alphabetizing*

warden (wôrd´ 'n)
waif (wāf)
waft (woft)
wanton (wont´ 'n)
wayfarer (wā´ fer´ ər)
wheedle (hwēd´ 'l)
winsome (win´ səm)
wraith (rāth)
withstand (with stand´)
whorl (hwôrl)

wean (wēn)
writhe (rīth)
wallop (wo´ ləp)
warble (wôr´ bəl)
welter (wel´ tər)
wieldy (wēl´ dē)
woeful (wō´ fəl)
wrath (rath)
wince (wins)
warrior (wôr´ ē ər)

Directions: Write the above vocabulary words in alphabetical order below.

1. waft
2. waif
3. wallop
4. wanton
5. warble
6. warden
7. warrior
8. wayfarer
9. wean
10. welter
11. wheedle
12. whorl
13. wieldy
14. wince
15. winsome
16. withstand
17. woeful
18. wraith
19. wrath
20. writhe

© Mark Twain Media, Inc., Publishers   89

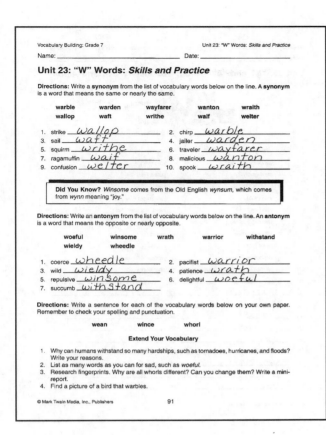

Name: _____ Date: _____

Unit 23: "W" Words: Skills and Practice

Directions: Write a **synonym** from the list of vocabulary words below on the line. A **synonym** is a word that means the same or nearly the same.

warble   warden   wayfarer   wanton   wraith
wallop   waft   writhe   waif   welter

1. strike _wallop_   2. chirp _warble_
3. sail _waft_   4. jailer _warden_
5. squirm _writhe_   6. traveler _wayfarer_
7. ragamuffin _waif_   8. malicious _wanton_
9. confusion _welter_   10. spook _wraith_

Did You Know? *Winsome* comes from the Old English *wynsum*, which comes from *wynn* meaning "joy."

Directions: Write an **antonym** from the list of vocabulary words below on the line. An **antonym** is a word that means the opposite or nearly opposite.

woeful   winsome   wrath   warrior   withstand
wieldy   wheedle

1. coerce _wheedle_   2. pacifist _warrior_
3. wild _wieldy_   4. patience _wrath_
5. repulsive _winsome_   6. delightful _woeful_
7. succumb _withstand_

Directions: Write a sentence for each of the vocabulary words below on your own paper. Remember to check your spelling and punctuation.

wean   wince   whorl

Extend Your Vocabulary

1. Why can humans withstand so many hardships, such as tornadoes, hurricanes, and floods? Write your reasons.
2. List as many words as you can for sad, such as *woeful*.
3. Research fingerprints. Why are all whorls different? Can you change them? Write a mini-report.
4. Find a picture of a bird that warbles.

© Mark Twain Media, Inc., Publishers   91

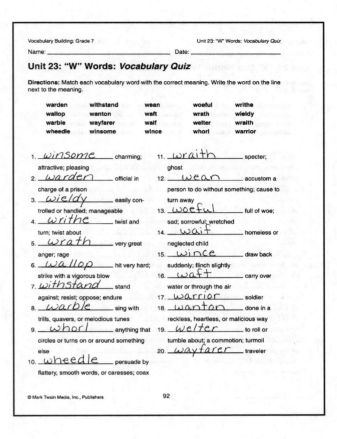

Name: _____ Date: _____

Unit 23: "W" Words: Vocabulary Quiz

Directions: Match each vocabulary word with the correct meaning. Write the word on the line next to the meaning.

warden   withstand   wean   woeful   writhe
wallop   wanton   waft   wrath   wieldy
warble   wayfarer   waif   welter   wraith
wheedle   winsome   wince   whorl   warrior

1. _winsome_ charming; attractive; pleasing
2. _warden_ official in charge of a prison
3. _wieldy_ easily controlled or handled; manageable
4. _writhe_ twist and turn; twist about
5. _wrath_ very great anger; rage
6. _wallop_ hit very hard; strike with a vigorous blow
7. _withstand_ stand against; resist; oppose; endure
8. _warble_ sing with trills, quavers, or melodious tunes
9. _whorl_ anything that circles or turns on or around something else
10. _wheedle_ persuade by flattery, smooth words, or caresses; coax
11. _wraith_ specter; ghost
12. _wean_ accustom a person to do without something; cause to turn away
13. _woeful_ full of woe; sad; sorrowful; wretched
14. _waif_ homeless or neglected child
15. _wince_ draw back suddenly; flinch slightly
16. _waft_ carry over water or through the air
17. _warrior_ soldier
18. _wanton_ done in a reckless, heartless, or malicious way
19. _welter_ to roll or tumble about; a commotion; turmoil
20. _wayfarer_ traveler

© Mark Twain Media, Inc., Publishers   92

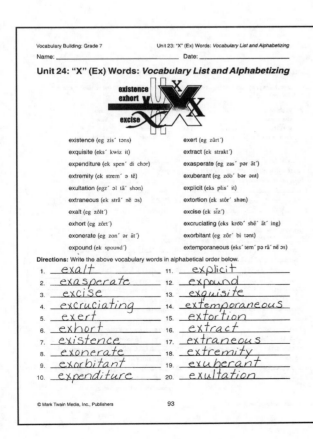

Name: _____ Date: _____

Unit 24: "X" (Ex) Words: Vocabulary List and Alphabetizing

existence
exhort
excise

existence (eg zis´ tɔns)   exert (eg zûrt´)
exquisite (eks´ kwiz it)   extract (ek strakt´)
expenditure (ek spen´ di chɔr)   exasperate (eg zas´ pɔr āt´)
extremity (ek strem´ ɔ tē)   exuberant (eg zōō´ bɔr ɔnt)
exultation (egz´ ɔl tā´ shɔn)   explicit (eks plis´ it)
extraneous (ek strā´ nē ɔs)   extortion (ek stôr´ shɔn)
exalt (eg zôlt´)   excise (ek sīz´)
exhort (eg zôrt´)   excruciating (eks krōō´ shē´ āt´ ing)
exonerate (eg zon´ ɔr āt´)   exorbitant (eg zôr´ bi tɔnt)
expound (ek spound´)   extemporaneous (eks´ tem´ pɔ rā´ nē ɔs)

Directions: Write the above vocabulary words in alphabetical order below.

1. _exalt_   11. _explicit_
2. _exasperate_   12. _expound_
3. _excise_   13. _exquisite_
4. _excruciating_   14. _extemporaneous_
5. _exert_   15. _extortion_
6. _exhort_   16. _extract_
7. _existence_   17. _extraneous_
8. _exonerate_   18. _extremity_
9. _exorbitant_   19. _exuberant_
10. _expenditure_   20. _exultation_

© Mark Twain Media, Inc., Publishers   93

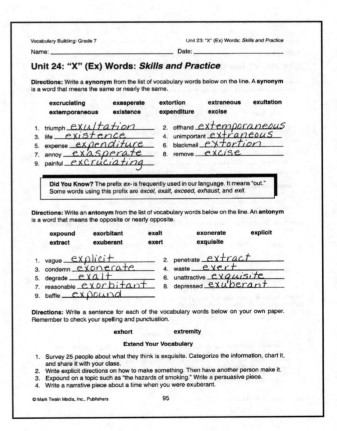

Name: _____ Date: _____

Unit 24: "X" (Ex) Words: Skills and Practice

Directions: Write a **synonym** from the list of vocabulary words below on the line. A **synonym** is a word that means the same or nearly the same.

excruciating   exasperate   extortion   extraneous   exultation
extemporaneous   existence   expenditure   excise

1. triumph _exultation_   2. offhand _extemporaneous_
3. life _existence_   4. unimportant _extraneous_
5. expense _expenditure_   6. blackmail _extortion_
7. annoy _exasperate_   8. remove _excise_
9. painful _excruciating_

Did You Know? The prefix *ex-* is frequently used in our language. It means "out." Some words using this prefix are *excel, exalt, exceed, exhaust,* and *exit.*

Directions: Write an **antonym** from the list of vocabulary words below on the line. An **antonym** is a word that means the opposite or nearly opposite.

expound   exorbitant   exalt   exonerate   explicit
extract   exuberant   exert   exquisite

1. vague _explicit_   2. penetrate _extract_
3. condemn _exonerate_   4. waste _exert_
5. degrade _exalt_   6. unattractive _exquisite_
7. reasonable _exorbitant_   8. depressed _exuberant_
9. baffle _expound_

Directions: Write a sentence for each of the vocabulary words below on your own paper. Remember to check your spelling and punctuation.

exhort   extremity

Extend Your Vocabulary

1. Survey 25 people about what they think is exquisite. Categorize the information, chart it, and share it with your class.
2. Write explicit directions on how to make something. Then have another person make it.
3. Expound on a topic such as "the hazards of smoking." Write a persuasive piece.
4. Write a narrative piece about a time when you were exuberant.

© Mark Twain Media, Inc., Publishers   95

Worksheet 1 (top left)

Unit 24: "X" (Ex) Words: *Vocabulary Quiz*

Directions: Match each vocabulary word with the correct meaning. Write the word on the line next to the meaning.

expenditure	existence	exquisite	extract	exert
exasperate	extremity	exuberant	exultation	exalt
excruciating	explicit	exonerate	extraneous	exhort
extemporaneous	extortion	exorbitant	expound	excise

1. *extortion* — obtaining by threats, force, fraud, or wrong use of authority
2. *exert* — put into use; use fully
3. *exonerate* — free from blame
4. *exultation* — an exulting; great rejoicing
5. *exalt* — make high in rank, honor, power, character, or quality; praise; glorify
6. *extract* — pull out or draw out, usually with some effort
7. *extraneous* — not essential
8. *extemporaneous* — spoken or done without preparation
9. *excruciating* — causing great suffering
10. *exquisite* — very lovely; delicate; most admirable
11. *excise* — cut out
12. *existence* — being; a being real
13. *exhort* — urge strongly; advise or warn earnestly
14. *expenditure* — using up; a spending
15. *exorbitant* — much too high; unreasonably excessive
16. *extremity* — the very end; farthest possible place; last point or part
17. *expound* — make clear; explain
18. *exasperate* — irritate very much; annoy greatly; make angry
19. *exuberant* — abounding in health and high spirits; overflowing with good cheer
20. *explicit* — clearly expressed; definite

96

Worksheet 2 (top right)

Unit 25: "Y" and "Z" Words: *Vocabulary List and Alphabetizing*

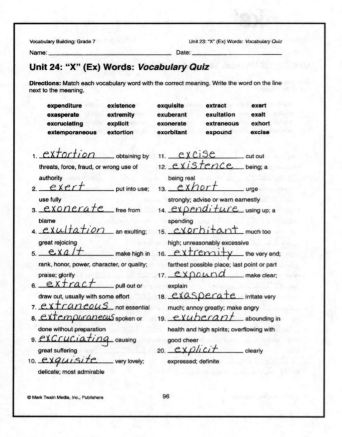

Zany, Yucca, Zealot, Yaws

yelp (yelp)	yeoman (yō´ mən)
yonder (yon´ dər)	yore (yôr)
yowl (youl)	yucca (yuk´ ə)
Yule (yōōl)	zany (zā´ nē)
yew (yōō)	yesteryear (yes´ tər yir´)
yen (yen)	zwieback (swī´ bak)
yearling (yir´ ling)	yawl (yôl)
zither (zith´ ər)	zealot (zel´ ət)
yaws (yôz)	yarrow (yar´ ō)
zephyr (zef´ ər)	yachtsman (yots´ mən)

Directions: Write the above vocabulary words in alphabetical order below.

1. yachtsman
2. yarrow
3. yawl
4. yaws
5. yearling
6. yelp
7. yen
8. yeoman
9. yesteryear
10. yew
11. yonder
12. yore
13. yowl
14. yucca
15. Yule
16. zany
17. zealot
18. zephyr
19. zither
20. zwieback

97

Worksheet 3 (bottom left)

Unit 25: "Y" and "Z" Words: *Skills and Practice*

Directions: Write a **synonym** from the list of vocabulary words below on the line. A **synonym** is a word that means the same or nearly the same.

yew	yore	yelp	yesteryear	zany
yawl	yowl	zealot	Yule	zephyr

1. Christmas *Yule*
2. last year *yesteryear*
3. fanatic *zealot*
4. bark *yelp*
5. long past *yore*
6. howl *yowl*
7. evergreen *yew*
8. foolish *zany*
9. boat *yawl*
10. breeze *zephyr*

> **Did You Know?** *Zwieback* is from German *zwieback*, meaning a "biscuit," which comes from *zwie*, meaning "twice," and *backen*, meaning "to bake."

Directions: Use the vocabulary words below to give an example(s) for each category. Write the word(s) on the line.

yaws	yen	zither	yucca	zwieback	yarrow

1. money *yen*
2. plant *yucca and yarrow*
3. disease *yaws*
4. instrument *zither*
5. toasted bread *zwieback*

Directions: Write a sentence for each of the vocabulary words below on your own paper. Remember to check for spelling and punctuation.

yeoman	yonder	yachtsman	yearling

Extend Your Vocabulary

1. List as many careers as you can that deal with the sea, such as yeoman and yachtsman.
2. Create a list of traditions you have at Yuletide. Compare with a friend.
3. Make a T-chart. Name plants or trees and their locations. For example: *yew - Europe, Asia* and *yucca - North and Central America.*
4. Write a narrative piece about a time when you were zany. Include where you were, who you were with, what happened, why it was zany, and how you felt.

99

Worksheet 4 (bottom right)

Unit 25: "Y" and "Z" Words: *Vocabulary Quiz*

Directions: Match each vocabulary word with the correct meaning. Write the word on the line next to the meaning.

yachtsman	yelp	yeoman	yonder	yore
yesteryear	yowl	yucca	yarrow	Yule
yearling	yew	yawl	yaws	yen
zwieback	zany	zealot	zither	zephyr

1. *yarrow* — common plant with finely divided leaves and flat clusters of white or pink flowers
2. *yelp* — quick, sharp bark or cry of a dog, fox, etc.
3. *yaws* — contagious disease of the tropics that produces sores on the skin
4. *yore* — long since gone
5. *yachtsman* — person who owns or sails a yacht
6. *Yule* — Yuletide; Christmas
7. *zealot* — person who shows too much zeal
8. *yen* — unit of money in Japan
9. *zwieback* — kind of bread or cake cut into slices and toasted dry in an oven
10. *yew* — evergreen tree native to Europe and Asia
11. *zany* — clownish; idiotic
12. *yowl* — long, distressful or dismal cry
13. *zither* — musical instrument having 30 or 40 strings, played with the fingers and a plectrum
14. *yonder* — within sight but not near; over there
15. *zephyr* — the west wind; strong, gentle breeze
16. *yucca* — plant found in dry, warm regions of North and Central America having stiff, narrow leaves at the base and an upright cluster of bell-shaped flowers
17. *yawl* — boat with a large mast near the bow and a small mast near the stern
18. *yesteryear* — last year; the year before this; in past years
19. *yearling* — one year old
20. *yeoman* — naval petty officer who performs clerical duties

100